W9-DCL-794

CODES and CIPHERS

by the same author
THE FACE OF WAR

CODES
and
CIPHERS

Secret Writing Through the Ages

by JOHN LAFFIN

illustrated by C. de la Nougerede

Abelard-Schuman
London   New York   Toronto

The author expresses his gratitude to Miss Hazelle Stonham, an accomplished professional cryptographer, for checking and correcting all examples and cryptograms in the book.

LONDON	NEW YORK	TORONTO
Abelard-Schuman	Abelard-Schuman	Abelard-Schuman
Limited	Limited	Canada Limited
8 King Street WC2	6 West 57 Street	896 Queen Street West

Printed in the United States of America

TO MY SON, CRAIG

Contents

Author's Note   11

1 Code and the Invasion of Europe; Cipher and the
  Downfall of a Traitor   19

2 Early Ciphers and Cryptographers; Caesar's Cipher;
  the Skytale; the Zodiac Alphabet; Abbot Trithemius   26

3 The Porta Table; the Vigenère Cipher; the Pig Pen
  Cipher   38

4 The Shakespeare — Bacon Argument   45

5 Cipher and Mary Queen of Scots; Shorthand; Brilliant
  Frenchmen; the Downfall of Monarchs; the Codes of
  Louis XIV   53

6 The Escape of Sir John Trevanion; Charles II's Cipher; An Error in Cipher makes a King; Diplomatic
  Double Talk   61

7 The Man in the Iron Mask   68

8 An American Code Book; Napoleon's Ciphers; Edgar
  Allan Poe; Major Kasiski and his Importance; Ciphers
  in the American Civil War; the Transatlantic Cable
  Row; Morse Code   72

9   Army Ciphers; Frustration for the Turks; Success for the French — the St. Cyr Cipher; the British Playfair Cipher; Lord Wolseley's Square; the Double Parallel Alphabet   80

10   Transposition Ciphers: some more Substitutions; the Two-step Cipher   88

11   Dots, Lines, Zigzags and Triangles; the Cipher Clock and the Cipher Machine; Symbol Codes   96

12   Colonel Redl Betrays his Country; the "Honorable" Seller of Codes; Austrian Success; General Hindenburg's Victory at the Battle of Tannenberg; the Russians Capture a Code; Room 40 of the Admiralty; the Zimmerman Telegram; German Ciphers   103

13   Transmitting Secret Writing; Ancient Methods; Hollow Teeth; Using the Post Office for Espionage; the Downfall of Spies; Invisible Ink; the Kent Case; the Black Chamber; Telepathy and Hypnosis   113

14   Mechanization: the Need for Speed   122

15   Frequencies; Occurrence of Bigrams; Most Commonly Doubled Letters in English; Useful Tips; Most Frequent Trigrams; Breaking Down a Cipher   127

16   Definitions   137

17   Some Cryptograms to Test your Skill   142

     Solutions   143

     Index   147

ILLUSTRATIONS

Tyronian Characters 28

The Skytale 30

Zodiac Alphabet 33

The Grille 36

The Pig-Pen Cipher 44

Shakespeare's Gravestone 51

Bright's Shorthand Alphabet 56

The Saint-Cyr Cipher 81

Zigzags, Lines, Dots, and Triangles 97

Cipher Clock 99

Criminals' Sign Writing 101

Author's Note

- **The Importance and Fascination of Code and Cipher**

THERE is a great need for this book for, fascinating though codes and ciphers are, cryptography is a neglected field in English. As recently as 1922, J. C. H. Macbeth, who translated a French book on cryptography into English, complained that there was no work on the subject in English. Mr. Macbeth wrote: "I have made a careful search, both in England and the United States, for a book or manual on this fascinating subject, but without success."

Since 1922 only two good books have appeared, plus some books of cryptograms. My book is intended for anybody interested in the stories behind the ciphers and codes of the last three thousand years. The very existence of a cipher emphasizes a great need for secrecy and where there is secrecy there is conflict and drama.

Codes and ciphers appear to be wrapped in so much

11

mystery that some people hesitate to tackle them. Yet they make a fascinating study and their historical background is full of drama and interest.

Codes and ciphers have changed the course of history and have played their part in great events. Many a famous battle and minor skirmish has been won or lost through ciphers; they have both caused and averted wars; they have carried across frontiers many dangerous secrets and, when broken, they have brought ruin to men and nations. They are used daily by every government in the world and are in more frequent use than most people realize.

Rulers have long used cryptography. King Alfred of England and Charlemagne of France used cryptography to communicate with their officers.

Now every government employs professional cryptographers — in the Foreign Office and State Department, in the Intelligence Department, the Army, the Navy and the Air Force. Scotland Yard and the F.B.I. have cipher and code experts on their staff, and other specialists work for big companies which have reason to keep their communications secret. Big firms use commercial codes which are not particularly interesting and are, therefore, not included in this book.

When the Head of a State or his Minister for Foreign Affairs leaves the country, he is always accompanied by experts from the Cipher Department.

Archaeologists are, by necessity, cryptanalysts because they frequently find on the urns, tombs and tablets of ancient races mysterious writings which they cannot decipher. Our knowledge of the civilization of ancient Persia would be practically nil, but for the greatest single work of decipherment ever carried out. Several men spent their lifetimes deciphering Persian inscriptions found on rocks. As one died another took his place and now, because of their painstaking work, anybody who wishes can decipher a Persian inscription.

Many a busy man, throughout the last hundred years especially, has found relaxation in the study of ciphers and codes as a hobby — a study which sharpens the brain and challenges wit, skill and patience. For years, I have kept up a correspondence in cipher with a friend in Canada. We send each other messages in cipher and we must break them, without knowing the key, to find out what each of us has written. This makes a letter much more interesting than usual.

I have mentioned the word cryptography. This is the form which covers the science of codes and ciphers and is derived from the Greek words *kryptos* (secret) and *graphos* (writing). In short, it is the art of sending a message in such a way that its hidden meaning is known only to the sender and the person for whom the message is intended — unless, of course, somebody else happens to break the message. And it is this third element that adds so much mystery and excitement to cryptography.

The word cipher means secret writing and comes from a Hebrew word, *saphar,* meaning "to number." To put it in the form of a simple definition, cipher is a method of secret writing that systematically disarranges the normal sequence of the letters of a plain text, or that substitutes other letters, characters or symbols for the normal alphabet.

Many people use the word "code" as if it were merely another word for cipher, but this is quite wrong. In a code a prearranged word may replace several words of the plain message or may even stand for the entire message. For instance, in one commercial code the word *agape* means *abandon negotiations.* But in a cipher every letter of the original message is replaced. A code is also a system of signals for communication by telegraph, such as Morse Code (which, as we shall see, is not a code but a cipher) or by semaphore, using signalling flags.

Anyone who knows the key of a cipher can read it without any equipment other than a pencil and paper. A code is not such a simple matter. Even when the key of a code is known, a code book or code dictionary is needed to translate the message. Some code books are enormous volumes.

There is another great difference between codes and ciphers. A cipher can express any thought whatever; a standard code can express nothing but the number of phrases in a code dictionary.

The prime disadvantage of a code is that the printing, distribution and possession of code books involves danger to security. And while a new cipher can be introduced at a moment's notice, much time is needed to prepare new code books.

A code does have some advantages over a cipher. A message is more rapidly encoded and decoded and needs less care. The breaking of a single cipher message exposes the whole system, but this is not necessarily true of a code.

Every navy uses codes. A code, because of its nature, poses tremendous problems for the enemy cryptanalyst and if he should partially obtain the solution, he is still no nearer solving the rest of the message. The limitations of a code book do not bother the Navy, for there is only a limited number of things a ship can be ordered to do.

Armies, however, use ciphers. Except for stationary or nearly stationary units, such as Army H.Q., army units cannot conveniently carry code dictionaries around with them, and, if they did, they might easily lose them to the enemy before they could be destroyed.

Warships have no such problem. Their code books are bound in lead, so that when thrown overboard — if capture appears imminent — they will sink at once.

Diplomats use both codes and ciphers, but prefer ciphers because they are more flexible and can express fine shades of meaning. Secret agents prefer codes because they can express more or less space, and a long message is dangerous to a spy. They prefer to give the impression that no message at all is being sent, hence the invention of invisible ink.

Criminals nearly always use ciphers, usually because the standard code books do not contain the particular phrases they want to use.

Probably the safest way of sending a message is to encipher a coded message. This double concealment could tax the ingenuity of even the most gifted cryptanalyst. Cryptography is an extremely old art. In ancient days, the ordinary written language was really secret writing, for very few people could read and write. Hence, if a general wanted to send a message to another general, he could simply write it in clear with very little risk of its being understood, if it should be captured. But when the ability to read and write became more commonplace, the necessity for a cipher arose.

The first certain appearance of the art was among the Greeks, who probably invented one of the two great types of ciphers — the transposition cipher, in which the letters of the original message were *rearranged* in some meaningless order.

Then, people of the late Roman Republic invented another great system, the substitution cipher, in which each letter of the clear was *replaced* by another letter, symbol or figure.

Naturally, we know more about the results of ciphers which have been broken than about those which have reached their destination successfully without being read by interceptors. People who have used a cipher successfully keep it secret and use it again. Therefore, the history of ciphers and codes is necessarily incomplete, but what we do know about them is sufficient to provide the basic material for many an adventurous fictional story. In fact, truth in code and cipher is often stranger than fiction.

John Laffin

CODES and CIPHERS

1

* **Code and the Invasion of Europe**
* **Cipher and the Downfall of a Traitor**

Codes and ciphers have had dramatic and exciting consequences for nations and for individuals.

In 1940, the Nazis of Germany overran Europe and for the next four years the conquered peoples hoped for an invasion by the British and Americans. The Germans expected an invasion, too, but they had so fortified the coast of Western Europe that they considered it impregnable. Nevertheless, German Intelligence kept trying to ferret out news of any projected attack. Code and cipher experts were particularly busy.

In January 1944, Admiral Canaris, Chief of German Intelligence, heard from an agent details of a strange two-part code signal which, so the agent said, the Allies would use to alert the French Resistance before the invasion of Europe.

Canaris warned his various Intelligence Groups that, in the months before D-Day, the Allies would send out hundreds of messages to the Resistance. But only a few would be genuinely related to D-Day; some would be fakes designed to confuse the Germans, while others would concern various Resistance activities.

The main German Intelligence Center listening to these messages was stationed near the Belgian border and was commanded by Lieutenant-Colonel Hellmuth Meyer. For months Meyer and his men listened to senseless messages — senseless, that is, to Meyer. Most of them meant something to the Resistance. There were such messages, in French, as "Molasses tomorrow will spurt out cognac"; "Pierre needs elastic for his braces"; "Sometimes the slowest horse wins." Meyer and his men, all cryptographers, were frustrated by their inability to decode these tantalizing messages.

On the night of June 1, 1944, after the 9 p.m. news broadcast by the B.B.C., the announcer began his usual preamble. "Kindly now listen to a few personal messages." A pause, then: "Les sanglots longs des violins de l'automne." (The long sobs of the violins of autumn — the first lines of a poem by Verlaine.)

The sergeant who recorded the message raced to Meyer. "The first part of the D-Day message has arrived!" he said excitedly. Perhaps he realized that the message was one of the most important code messages ever sent.

Meyer played the record over twice. There was no mistaking the message; and it warned the Resistance that the invasion was imminent. According to the information Canaris had received, there would be a second message — "Blessent mon coeur d'une langueur monotone." (Wound my heart with a monotonous languor — further lines from the same poem.) This would warn the Resistance that the invasion would begin within forty-eight hours, the count to start from midnight of the day following the broadcast. As it happened, the message was repeated the next two nights. Meyer passed on the information, but few senior commanders acted on it.

Between June 1-6, many code messages relating to D-Day were sent to the Resistance, but two are especially interesting. "It is hot in Suez," was an order to the men of the underground to sabotage railway tracks and trains. The other, "The dice are on the table," told them to cut telephone lines and cables.

Meanwhile, Lieutenant-Colonel Meyer waited tensely for the second part of the message. He knew how vital it was for him to pick up the message and send it on. If the Germans acted in time, they could stop the invasion on the beaches.

At 10:15 on the night of June 5, the waiting men in Meyer's Intelligence Center heard the impersonal voice of the B.B.C. announcer say: "Blessent mon coeur d'une langueur monotone."

It was probably the most exciting moment experienced by any cryptographers of either side, during World War II. These professional experts in codes and ciphers had the first information of the most massive invasion in history. Meyer, at least, knew he was taking part in cryptographic history.

Unfortunately for the Germans, not all the senior officers really believed that an invasion was possible, and the information was ignored, but no blame for the German defeat can be laid on the cryptographers. Throughout the war they served their country well, as cryptographers of all nations have done. The Germans were true to a long tradition.

An individual drastically affected by ciphers was the Chevalier René de Rohan who, in 1674, commanded the French town of Quilleboeuf on the Dutch frontier. The Chevalier frequently boasted of his ability with ciphers. He could break any cipher, he claimed, although genuine experts never boast about their skill; sometimes a simple cipher is difficult to break. But de Rohan was a braggart, and worse, he was a traitor.

The Dutch, the enemies of the French at this time, knew that de Rohan could be bought and they offered him a good price to betray the town to them. The Chevalier hesitated at first — not because of his honor, however. He wanted more money. Finally the Dutch agreed to his price and his assistant, de Truaumont, also a traitor, was sent to get the cash.

When he brought it back, the French Secret Service — which was not as inefficient as de Rohan had believed — pounced on both men, and locked them in separate cells. The Chevalier spent a few fearful days, dreading the death he knew he must now expect.

He refused to confess to treason and, from the questions of his interrogators, he knew that they had no positive proof against him. The only man who could prove treason was de Truaumont, and if he did not talk, de Rohan felt fairly safe. But even a strong man could be made to talk under torture, and it was certainly safe to assume that de Truaumont was being tortured.

One day, de Rohan received a parcel of clothing sent to him by his friends. He was sure that in it he would find a message of hope, perhaps even a plan of escape. Sure enough, on the sleeve of a shirt he found this cipher message:

MG EULHXCCLGU GHJ YXUJ LM CT ULGC ALJ.

For years, de. Rohan had bragged that he could solve any cipher message and his friends had taken him at his word. Now, he had before him one that was vital to him — and he could make nothing of it. He scribbled away at possible solutions and produced nothing that made any more sense than the original. Hours of such work can tire even a well-balanced brain — and de Rohan's was too frantic with worry to be well-balanced. He still had not solved the cipher when he was taken from his cell to face the judges at his trial. Completely broken, he poured out his confession and a few hours later was hanged — a miserable weakling of a man.

His friends were astounded at his confession. They had sent him a message telling him in almost as many words that he was safe, and that de Truaumont had refused to speak. In fact, de Truaumont had been cruelly treated but, even if he had not been loyal to his country, he was faithful to his friend, de Rohan.

This was what the message had told de Rohan, the "in-

fallible expert" in ciphers. It was such a simple cipher message — MG EULHXCCLGU GHJ YXUJ LM CT ULGC ALJ. This is
merely a substitution cipher for *Le prisonnier est mort; il
n'a rien dit.* (In English: *The prisoner is dead: he said
nothing.*)

If you had received the cipher message, this is how you
would have easily deciphered it:

Taking a count of the letters, we find that the letters C,
G and H each occur four times, so one of the three is almost
certainly E — the most common letter in most languages.
G is the most likely to represent E, for it appears last in
Group 1, a two-letter group, and the word LE (the) is one
of the commonest in French. G is also in the first position
in Group 3, and reference to the Frequency Tables (see
page 129) shows that the word EST (is) is also very common. Assuming that G equals E, and that M equals L, H
equals S and J equals T, we could have the following:

LE ‖ _ _ _ S _ _ _ _ E _ ‖ EST ‖ _ _ _ T ‖ _ L ‖ _ _ ‖

            _ _ E _ ‖ _ _ T.

Group 5 must be the word IL (he), so assuming L to stand
for I, we have:

LE ‖ _ _ IS _ _ _ IER ‖ EST ‖ _ _ _ T ‖ IL ‖ _ _ ‖ _ IE _ ‖ _ IT.

It is a fair assumption that Group 7 must be the word
RIEN (nothing). And if C stands for N, we have found out
two more letters:

LE ‖ _ RIS _ NNIER ‖ EST ‖ _ _ RT ‖

            IL ‖ N _ ‖ RIEN ‖ _ IT.

It does not take much thinking to fill in the remaining blanks — E equals P, X equals O, Y equals M, A equals D, and T equals A. All this shows that anybody interested in cryptography must be reasonably familiar with the Frequency Tables. Had de Rohan been the expert he claimed to be, he would have known them backwards.

It has been like this down through the ages with the safety of nations and the lives of men depending on codes and ciphers.

2

- **Early Ciphers and Cryptographers**
- **Caesar's Cipher**
- **The Skytale**
- **The Zodiac Alphabet**
- **Abbot Trithemius**

FROM the very first, all ciphers have been based on two fundamental principles — transposition and substitution. The only other possibility is to combine the two. These principles must be clearly understood before any study of ciphers is possible.

Transposition ciphers are formed merely by changing the normal position of the units that form the clear message. Most people, at some time or another, have written a sentence backwards or the letters of each word in a sentence backwards. TEEM OUY TA RUOF. (Meet you at four.) This is a simple transposition cipher.

Letters can be rearranged in an extraordinary number of ways. Three letters, such as the word "the", can be written six different ways: THE, TEH, HET, HTE, ETH, EHT. A group of twenty letters could be arranged in 2,432,902,-007,246,400,000 ways.

André Langie, a famous French cryptographer, worked

out that a cryptanalyst devoting a second to each combination would finish his work in 75,000,000,000 years.

In short, in a transposition cipher the letters remain the same as in the clear, but are shuffled according to a prearranged pattern. The correspondents could decide to send a message — STAY AWAY — *in two lines*:

S A   A A

T Y   W Y

The message would be enciphered SAAA TYWY.

In a substitution cipher, the letters of the clear are replaced by letters, figures or symbols. In its simplest form, one letter of the clear is represented by one, and always the same, letter, figure or symbol. We decide, for example, that each letter of the clear will be represented by the one preceding it in the alphabet. To encipher STAY AWAY, we would write: RSZX ZVZX.

Later we will see how, by using a two-step cipher, transposition and substitution may be combined.

One of Julius Caesar's many achievements was his invention of a very rudimentary form of substitution cipher. All he did was to move each letter of the clear three places down the alphabet. So that if he wanted to send the message ATTACK, he would send the cipher DWWDFN, though his cipher would not have been exactly this because some modern letters did not exist in the Roman alphabet.

This cipher, which is so simple as to be positively dangerous, is still known as the Julius Caesar Cipher, but Caesar himself soon abandoned it for he did not trust Cicero, with whom he had shared the secret of the cipher.

Cicero himself had his scribe, Tyro, invent some secret writing which looks remarkably like modern shorthand. Tyro worked very hard at the secret writing because Cicero promised him his freedom if his method stood up against attempts at decipherment. Tyro evolved some strange characters, still known as Tyronian characters. This is what some of them looked like:

AℓC = AUGUSTUS   **ː6** = EMPEROR

Tyronian Characters

Another early exponent of cipher was the great Lysander of Sparta. In 405 B.C., Lysander won the sea battle of Aegospotami against the Athenians, but for the next year he was worried and fearful, for he was surrounded by false friends and traitors. One false move and he and Sparta would be lost. Lysander trusted nobody and especially he distrusted a leading Persian, Pharnabazus, whom he suspected of plotting against him.

Lysander had a fearful problem. Should he attack Persia or not? Was Persia friend or foe? If he waited for Persia to attack first, he would lose the battle. But if Persia was an ally, as Pharnabazus claimed she was, then to attack her would be a grave mistake.

One summer afternoon, a year after Aegospotami, Lysander was pacing restlessly in his garden, from where he could hear the crowd calling his name in praise. Then, suddenly, two soldiers dragged into his presence a tattered, exhausted man, caked in blood and filth. Tearing himself away from the soldiers, the man rushed at Lysander.

"I have travelled far and dangerously," he panted. "I am the only one of five who set out to reach you."

"Silence!" Lysander said and ordered the soldiers to leave the garden. When they had gone, he turned again to the messenger. "Give me your belt!" he said.

The man took off his long leather belt, down one edge of which was a series of meaningless letters. From his own belt Lysander took a cylindrical staff, known as a skytale. Through a slit on the left-hand side of the cylinder, Lysander threaded the messenger's belt and wound it around and around the skytale, spiral fashion.

When he had made the last turn, the hidden meaning of the message was clear. It was an important cipher, revealing Pharnabazus's treachery. He had killed Lysander's closest friend and had brought charges against Lysander himself. Lysander mobilized at once, and within hours his galleys were *en route* to battle — and victory against the Persians. This victory was important to world history; it led to the final overthrow of the East by the West.

A skytale is easy to make with a pencil and strip of paper about a foot long and an inch-and-a-half wide. Wrap the paper around the pencil, winding it toward you, and broadly overlapping it. Keep the paper firmly in place

The Skytale

and write your message on it in six lines of nine letters.
Suppose your message is:

I CANNOT TRAVEL FURTHER WITHOUT STRONG
REINFORCEMENTS AND GUNS

Divide this message into six lines and write them in sequence around the pencil. Write each of the nine letters
on each of the nine turns of the spiral. You will have this:

I	C	A	N	N	O	T	T	R
A	V	E	L	F	U	R	T	H
E	R	W	I	T	H	O	U	T
S	T	R	O	N	G	R	E	I
N	F	O	R	C	E	M	E	N
T	S	A	N	D	G	U	N	S

Now unwind the strip and you will have a line of un-
connected letters on the left-hand edge. If you send this
to a friend in on the secret, he would roll the strip round a
skytale of exactly the same size and the message would
be instantly readable.

You need to remember that the larger the diameter of
the skytale, the fewer the number of turns in the spiral.

This means that it will be possible to write many more lines but that these lines will contain only as many letters as there are turns.

The early Greeks often used figure ciphers, by squaring the alphabet, as shown below, and numbering each horizontal and vertical row from one to five. If we were to use this method, we would have to omit one letter and that usually left out is J; I does duty both for itself and J. Alternatively, U and V can do double duty.

	1	2	3	4	5
1	A	F	L	Q	V
2	B	G	M	R	W
3	C	H	N	S	X
4	D	I	O	T	Y
5	E	K	P	U	Z

To encipher a letter, show the numbers of the intersecting rows, giving first the number of the vertical column. For instance, A is 11 and O becomes 43. Decipher this message: 23-43-24-51-23 43-33-51-45-33 51-51-41-51-41 11-44-43-33-31-51-. MORE MONEY NEEDED AT ONCE. (Normally, the cipher would be written down in groups of five figures: 23432 45123 43335, etc).

Despite the use the Greeks, Romans, Venetians and others made of cryptography, the art went into eclipse for many centuries and was not really revived until the Middle Ages. During the early Middle Ages, picture alphabets — looking very mysterious to the uninitiated — were popular in cipher work. One of the most popular was the Zodiac Alphabet, shown on the facing page.

The signs represent the best-known heavenly bodies. Others — such as the Twins, the Balance, the Ram and so on — are still used by astrologers who claim to be able to predict events by the position of the stars. The signs for w, x, y and z are merely to complete the alphabet. In the Middle Ages, when few people were educated and most were superstitious, anybody who happened to come upon a message written in these characters would probably be vastly impressed with the learning of the man who had penned them, and would never suspect that they cloaked a sinister message.

The latter years of the 14th century were important for Europe. There was much chaos and confusion, plotting and scheming, death and destruction — but in the midst of it all there was some brightness as questing men began to strive towards culture and learning. Standards of living began to improve and trade between countries to increase. Inevitably there was rivalry, both peaceful and violent, and men needed some way of sending news quickly and secretly. This need resulted in improved ciphers.

In 1499, a Benedictine abbot named Trithemius, who lived in Spanheim in Germany, wrote the first book on cryptography. The book, called *Polygraphia*, was printed in Latin, but a few years later it appeared in German and French, indication enough of its need.

Much of Abbot Trithemius's book was pretty poor stuff by modern standards. But he did evolve a clever cipher system by drawing up a set of fourteen alphabets in which letters were replaced by words or phrases.

One such alphabet runs like this:

A *In heavens*
B *Ever & Ever*
C *World   without End*
D *In one infinity*
E *Perpetuity*
F *Sempiternal*
G *Enduring*
H *Incessantly*
I, J *Irreversibly*
K *Eternally*
L *In glory*
M *In the light*
N *In Paradise*
O *Always*
P *In Divinity*
Q *In Deity*
R *In felicity*
S *In His Reign*
T *In   His   Kingdom*
U, V, W *In beatitude*
X *In His Magnificence*
Y *To the throne*
Z *In all eternity*

A = ⊙ SUN		N = ♌ LION
B = ♃ JUPITER		O = ♍ VIRGO
C = ♄ SATURN		P = ♎ BALANC
D = ♆ NEPTUNE		Q = ♏ SCORPIO
E = ♅ URANUS		R = ↗ SAGITTAR
F = ♁ EARTH		S = ♑ CAPRICORN
G = ♀ VENUS		T = ♓ FISHES
H = ♂ MARS		U = ♈ RAM
I = ☿ MERCURY		V = ♒ AQUARIUS
J = ☾ MOON		W = >
K = ♉ TAURUS		X = ≫
L = ♊ TWINS		Y = ⊣
M = ♋ CANCER		Z = <

Zodiac Alphabet

If the Abbot wanted to encode the plea SEND HELP, he would write: IN HIS REIGN [in] PERPETUITY [and] IN PARADISE [in] ONE INFINITY INCESSANTLY [for] PERPETUITY [and] IN GLORY [and] IN DIVINITY.

The addition of the words in brackets, to make the message read more fluidly, would not confuse the recipient of the message who had copies of the alphabets. The sender could choose words and phrases from any of the fourteen alphabets and would quote the number of the alphabet from which they came. The disadvantage of the system was the time taken to write a long message.

The advantages of the Trithemian system are that even the existence of a ciphered message can be concealed; the clear may be in one language and the message in another; and, because of the many equivalents, decipherers would have to accumulate a lot of material before they could hope to find similarities which might lead to their breaking the cipher.

Unfortunately for the Abbot, many people who read his book accused him of black magic. This led to such a fuss that all copies of the book that could be rounded up were publicly burned. The Abbot was lucky that he was not burned with them.

An Italian doctor (Jeronimo Cardano) followed Abbot Trithemius as the next important cryptographer. Cardano invented the Trellis (or Grille) Cipher, which is still used in various forms. A grille is simply a piece of paper with a number of holes cut in it. To write a secret message, you put the grille over a sheet of writing paper and through the holes you put down the letters which make up the message. Then you take away the grille and compose a longer message around the key letters. The recipient, who has an identical grille, simply puts it over the message and at once the secret communication is revealed. Suppose we take the short message: ESCAPE AT ONCE. We need a grille of twelve letters, that is, twelve small squares cut at random in the grille-paper, and numbered.

Write through these windows the letters of the message. When you remove the grille, the letters are ar-

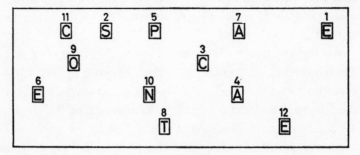

The Grille

ranged meaninglessly. We write a message, any message, around the letters, so as to make it appear a harmless letter. But the recipient has only to put his own grille over the letter to see what it contains.

3

- **The Porta Table**
- **The Vigenère Cipher**
- **The Pig Pen Cipher**

History has given the title of Father of Modern Cryptography to an Italian, Giovanni Baptista della Porta. Some critics subsequently decried della Porta, but his system, published in Naples in 1565, was efficient on all counts. The Porta Table is shown on facing page.

The capital letters on the left form the key agreed upon, the letters of which indicate, in succession, the alphabets selected. Each pair of capitals controls the alphabet arranged in two lines on their right. Simply, we want to encipher the letter *e* by using the key letter k. In the alphabet which k controls, the letter *z* falls under *e*; *z*, then, is the cipher letter.

A longer example: The clear message is CHIEF LEAVES ON SUNDAY. Key word: MISTER.

The first cipher letter is w, representing C. You could

THE PORTA TABLE

A B	*a*	*b*	*c*	*d*	*e*	*f*	*g*	*h*	*i*	*j*	*k*	*l*	*m*
	n	*o*	*p*	*q*	*r*	*s*	*t*	*u*	*v*	*w*	*x*	*y*	*z*

C D	*a*	*b*	*c*	*d*	*e*	*f*	*g*	*h*	*i*	*j*	*k*	*l*	*m*
	z	*n*	*o*	*p*	*q*	*r*	*s*	*t*	*u*	*v*	*w*	*x*	*y*

E F	*a*	*b*	*c*	*d*	*e*	*f*	*g*	*h*	*i*	*j*	*k*	*l*	*m*
	y	*z*	*n*	*o*	*p*	*q*	*r*	*s*	*t*	*u*	*v*	*w*	*x*

G H	*a*	*b*	*c*	*d*	*e*	*f*	*g*	*h*	*i*	*j*	*k*	*l*	*m*
	x	*y*	*z*	*n*	*o*	*p*	*q*	*r*	*s*	*t*	*u*	*v*	*w*

I J	*a*	*b*	*c*	*d*	*e*	*f*	*g*	*h*	*i*	*j*	*k*	*l*	*m*
	w	*x*	*y*	*z*	*n*	*o*	*p*	*q*	*r*	*s*	*t*	*u*	*v*

K L	*a*	*b*	*c*	*d*	*e*	*f*	*g*	*h*	*i*	*j*	*k*	*l*	*m*
	v	*w*	*x*	*y*	*z*	*n*	*o*	*p*	*q*	*r*	*s*	*t*	*u*

M N	*a*	*b*	*c*	*d*	*e*	*f*	*g*	*h*	*i*	*j*	*k*	*l*	*m*
	u	*v*	*w*	*x*	*y*	*z*	*n*	*o*	*p*	*q*	*r*	*s*	*t*

O P	*a*	*b*	*c*	*d*	*e*	*f*	*g*	*h*	*i*	*j*	*k*	*l*	*m*
	t	*u*	*v*	*w*	*x*	*y*	*z*	*n*	*o*	*p*	*q*	*r*	*s*

Q R	*a*	*b*	*c*	*d*	*e*	*f*	*g*	*h*	*i*	*j*	*k*	*l*	*m*
	s	*t*	*u*	*v*	*w*	*x*	*y*	*z*	*n*	*o*	*p*	*q*	*r*

S T	*a*	*b*	*c*	*d*	*e*	*f*	*g*	*h*	*i*	*j*	*k*	*l*	*m*
	r	*s*	*t*	*u*	*v*	*w*	*x*	*y*	*z*	*n*	*o*	*p*	*q*

U V	*a*	*b*	*c*	*d*	*e*	*f*	*g*	*h*	*i*	*j*	*k*	*l*	*m*
	q	*r*	*s*	*t*	*u*	*v*	*w*	*x*	*y*	*z*	*n*	*o*	*p*

W X	*a*	*b*	*c*	*d*	*e*	*f*	*g*	*h*	*i*	*j*	*k*	*l*	*m*
	p	*q*	*r*	*s*	*t*	*u*	*v*	*w*	*x*	*y*	*z*	*n*	*o*

Y Z	*a*	*b*	*c*	*d*	*e*	*f*	*g*	*h*	*i*	*j*	*k*	*l*	*m*
	o	*p*	*q*	*r*	*s*	*t*	*u*	*v*	*w*	*x*	*y*	*z*	*n*

THE VIGENÈRE TABLE

CAPITALS REPRESENTING KEY LETTERS

	A	B	C	D	E	F	G	H	I	J	K	L	M	N	O	P	Q	R	S	T	U	V	W	X	Y	Z
A	a	b	c	d	e	f	g	h	i	j	k	l	m	n	o	p	q	r	s	t	u	v	w	x	y	z
B	b	c	d	e	f	g	h	i	j	k	l	m	n	o	p	q	r	s	t	u	v	w	x	y	z	a
C	c	d	e	f	g	h	i	j	k	l	m	n	o	p	q	r	s	t	u	v	w	x	y	z	a	b
D	d	e	f	g	h	i	j	k	l	m	n	o	p	q	r	s	t	u	v	w	x	y	z	a	b	c
E	e	f	g	h	i	j	k	l	m	n	o	p	q	r	s	t	u	v	w	x	y	z	a	b	c	d
F	f	g	h	i	j	k	l	m	n	o	p	q	r	s	t	u	v	w	x	y	z	a	b	c	d	e
G	g	h	i	j	k	l	m	n	o	p	q	r	s	t	u	v	w	x	y	z	a	b	c	d	e	f
H	h	i	j	k	l	m	n	o	p	q	r	s	t	u	v	w	x	y	z	a	b	c	d	e	f	g
I	i	j	k	l	m	n	o	p	q	r	s	t	u	v	w	x	y	z	a	b	c	d	e	f	g	h
J	j	k	l	m	n	o	p	q	r	s	t	u	v	w	x	y	z	a	b	c	d	e	f	g	h	i
K	k	l	m	n	o	p	q	r	s	t	u	v	w	x	y	z	a	b	c	d	e	f	g	h	i	j
L	l	m	n	o	p	q	r	s	t	u	v	w	x	y	z	a	b	c	d	e	f	g	h	i	j	k
M	m	n	o	p	q	r	s	t	u	v	w	x	y	z	a	b	c	d	e	f	g	h	i	j	k	l
N	n	o	p	q	r	s	t	u	v	w	x	y	z	a	b	c	d	e	f	g	h	i	j	k	l	m
O	o	p	q	r	s	t	u	v	w	x	y	z	a	b	c	d	e	f	g	h	i	j	k	l	m	n
P	p	q	r	s	t	u	v	w	x	y	z	a	b	c	d	e	f	g	h	i	j	k	l	m	n	o
Q	q	r	s	t	u	v	w	x	y	z	a	b	c	d	e	f	g	h	i	j	k	l	m	n	o	p
R	r	s	t	u	v	w	x	y	z	a	b	c	d	e	f	g	h	i	j	k	l	m	n	o	p	q
S	s	t	u	v	w	x	y	z	a	b	c	d	e	f	g	h	i	j	k	l	m	n	o	p	q	r
T	t	u	v	w	x	y	z	a	b	c	d	e	f	g	h	i	j	k	l	m	n	o	p	q	r	s
U	u	v	w	x	y	z	a	b	c	d	e	f	g	h	i	j	k	l	m	n	o	p	q	r	s	t
V	v	w	x	y	z	a	b	c	d	e	f	g	h	i	j	k	l	m	n	o	p	q	r	s	t	u
W	w	x	y	z	a	b	c	d	e	f	g	h	i	j	k	l	m	n	o	p	q	r	s	t	u	v
X	x	y	z	a	b	c	d	e	f	g	h	i	j	k	l	m	n	o	p	q	r	s	t	u	v	w
Y	y	z	a	b	c	d	e	f	g	h	i	j	k	l	m	n	o	p	q	r	s	t	u	v	w	x
Z	z	a	b	c	d	e	f	g	h	i	j	k	l	m	n	o	p	q	r	s	t	u	v	w	x	y

CAPITALS REPRESENTING CLEAR LETTERS

complete it for yourself. The complete cipher: wQzvQ QYW-
EVH JG JDJOSE.

Despite della Porta's importance, a French nobleman,
Blaise de Vigenère, has much better claim to the title of
Father of Modern Cryptography.

The Frenchman flourished during the reign of Henry III.
A nobleman, he had various posts in the diplomatic service until, at the age of forty, he went back to school to
study weighty books in Greek, Hebrew and Latin, in an
effort to learn how to make gold.

He was unsuccessful and, after four years' work, he was
recalled to Government service and sent to Rome on a
diplomatic mission. While in Rome, he happened to read
della Porta's book on cryptography and became so fasci-
nated with the subject that he set out to become a cryptographer. In fact, he spent so much time on the subject that
he neglected his professional duties. After a lot of study
and work, de Vigenère produced a cipher which he
claimed was indecipherable. This is always a rash claim
but, as it happened, de Vigenère's cipher, an improvement
on della Porta's system, was to remain unbreakable for
many years.

The great advantage of de Vigenère's table, as it came
to be called, was its simplicity. By using the table, we can
encipher a message quickly and easily. Suppose we want
to encipher MONEY NEEDED URGENTLY. First of all, we need
a key word, which can be of any length provided it does
not contain any letter twice. We will take SAFE as the key
word. We now write out our message with the key word
repeated over it as many times as necessary.

Key word:
S A F E S   A F E S A F   E S A F E S A F

Message:
M O N E Y   N E E D E D   U R G E N T L Y

The first letter to be enciphered is the M of MONEY,
which comes beneath s of the key word SAFE. Looking at
the Vigenère table, we find M in the capital alphabet representing Clear Letters and s in the capital alphabet
standing for Key Letters. Follow each of these two lines
along until they meet; they meet at E. Therefore, in our
cipher, M is replaced by E. The next letter of the clear,
O, coincides with A of the key word, which gives us O on
the table, as well. The full cipher will be:

EOSIQ NJIVEI YJGJRLLD

But we can make this even more baffling, by changing
the grouping, say, to this: EOS IQNJI VEIY JGJ RLLD.

An expert could solve the puzzle without knowing the
key word, but it would take time and give him a head-
ache. With the key word, a message can quickly be deciphered. You can prove this by deciphering the code
word WNLPSNI, using the key word SAFE. The first letter
W falls under the s of SAFE. Find s in the key letter capitals and follow this line down until you come to w. w is
in the line of clear-letter capitals beginning with E, so w
must equal E. E is the first letter of the enciphered word.

The Vigenère Cipher has some interesting variations.
In one of the most commonly used, the Autoclave Cipher,

a key letter is used instead of a key word. Suppose the key letter is в and we want to encipher the brief instruction RETURN. We encipher the first letter, R, with the key letter, B. On the Vigenère table, we find that в and R intersect at s, which becomes the first cipher letter. s now becomes the key letter for us to encipher E, the second letter of the clear. s and E intersect at w. As you can see, each letter of the cipher is used as the key letter for the next letter of the clear. Finally, for RETURN, we have SWPJAN. A message can be enciphered very quickly by this system.

Another Vigenère system uses a key number, such as 3721. Our message is:

MONEY SENT

Key number:	3	2	7	1	3	2	7	1	3
	M	O	N	E	Y	S	E	N	T

The figure 3 appears over the first letter of the clear, so we move it three places along the alphabet. That is, M becomes P. Figure 2 appears over O, we move it two places along to Q. Our complete cipher will read: PQUFB ULOWX. The X, of course, is a null. It is always best to use letters of reasonable frequency as nulls for the simple reason that they are not obviously nulls. X and Z are quickly recognized as nulls. However, I have used X throughout this book so as to make the use of a null more easily identifiable. This cipher also enables quick enciphering and deciphering.

One method commonly in use before the Renaissance

was the Pig-Pen Cipher. Baptista della Porta developed a version of it and some secret societies used it as late as 1600. The Pig-Pen Cipher was used during the American Civil War by Union prisoners in Confederate jails to send messages to friends outside. Many schoolboys use it today.

A	B	C	D	E	F	G	H	I
J	K	L	M	N	O	P	Q	R
S	T	U	V	W	X	Y	Z	

The following cipher means: THOMPSON HAS A BIG CHOCOLATE.

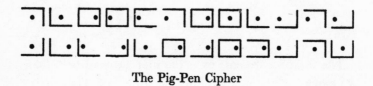

The Pig-Pen Cipher

Here is a variation of the same cipher:

A	E	D		L		N	Q	R		Y
F	I	H	K		M	S	T	U	X	Z
B	G	C		J		O	V	P		W

4

Cryptographers have made some fascinating claims relating to history. Some, for instance, have discovered ciphers in the literary works of the famous Elizabethan, Francis Bacon, Lord Verulam — Lord Chancellor during the reign of Elizabeth I — which, they claim, prove that he wrote the works attributed to Shakespeare, and that Bacon was the son of Queen Elizabeth and the Earl of Leicester.

I have yet to be convinced that either of these claims is valid, but it is true that Bacon was a cryptographer and, in fact, he invented a cipher alphabet in which the two letters, A and B, in various combinations, stand for all twenty-six letters of the clear alphabet.

A   *aaaaa*
B   *aaaab*
C   *aaaba*
D   *aaabb*
E   *aabaa*
F   *aabab*
G   *aabba*
H   *aabbb*
IJ   *abaaa*
K   *abaab*
L   *ababa*
M   *ababb*
N   *abbaa*
O   *abbab*
P   *abbba*
Q   *abbbb*
R   *baaaa*
S   *baaab*
T   *baaba*
UV   *baabb*
W   *babaa*
X   *babab*
Y   *babba*
Z   *babbb*

Using this cipher, we would encipher *England* as *aabaa-abbaaaabbaabababaaaaaabbaaaaabb*. Deciphering a message in the Baconian cipher would try the patience of even the most painstaking cryptographer!

Bacon was devoted to cipher, and wrote much about the subject. "A perfect cipher," he wrote, "must be not laborious to write and read; it must be impossible to decipher; and, in some cases, it must be without suspicion."

Despite this, Bacon's own bilateral cipher is extremely laborious. It had to be printed in two different types with a scarcely discernible difference and a message could be deciphered, even by the intended recipient, only by a complicated, time-wasting process.

It was largely Bacon's interest in cipher that fed the claims that he was the real author of the Shakespearean plays. Horace Walpole was probably the first to make this claim, but it is doubtful if Walpole was serious. Certainly, many people who repeated the claim after him only did so for fun. Then, in 1848, an English writer, J. G. Hart, wrote a serious book about Bacon's claims. Other advocates of the Hart school claimed that only a lawyer — and Bacon was one — could have written the plays.

It was an American politician, Ignatius T. Donnelly, who, in the 1870's, went to work to find cipher messages in the plays. He began by checking the occurrences of the word "bacon" in the plays, though this, of course, proved nothing. In two years of hard work, Donnelly worked out a complete system of decipherment — at least to his own satisfaction. He published all his complicated findings in a book called *The Great Cryptogram*.

Donnelly was no cryptographer, and his book was criticized caustically by several people who were. They
pointed out that Donnelly had simply worked out a cipher
to fit his own beliefs. One cryptographer supported his
criticisms by "proving" facetiously that Shakespeare had
written the Forty-Sixth Psalm. The psalm is numbered
46; the 46th word from the beginning is "shake"; the 46th
word from the end is "spear." Conclusion: Shakespeare
wrote it.

Under the attack, Donnelly retired from the scene, but
other Bacon supporters took up the fight. One of the most
prominent was an American, Dr. Robert Dale Owen, who
worked out another decipherment which he published as
Sir Francis Bacon's Cipher Story. This impressed professional cryptographers no more than had Donnelly's book.

At this point, Mrs. Elizabeth Gallup, Owen's secretary,
published a book of her own, *The Bilateral Cipher of
Francis Bacon,* in which she claimed that Bacon's famous
bilateral system — the two founts with their combinations
of the letters "a" and "b" — proved him to be the author
of the plays. Her case was thorough and plausible, even if
her conclusions were startling.

Mrs. Gallup said that Queen Elizabeth, in her youth,
had married the Earl of Leicester, and that they had a
child, known as Francis Bacon. A second child was known
as the Earl of Essex. Bacon had not dared claim his in-
heritance, but Essex did and finished on the scaffold. In
fact, he was persecuted by his brother, Bacon, on the
Queen's orders. She was determined to convince him that

it would be unsafe for him to make any claim on his own behalf.

In the first edition of Shakespeare's works, published by Isaac Jaggard in 1623, Mrs. Gallup claimed to have found the following message, enciphered in the L. Digges' Poem.

"Francis of Verulam is the author of all the plays heretofore published by Marlowe, Greene, Peele and Shakespeare, and of the twenty-two (plays) now put out for the first time. Some are altered to continue his history. Fr. St. A."

Further, Mrs. Gallup claimed, Bacon was also the real author of the works supposedly written by Robert Burton, Ben Jonson, and Edmund Spenser. Bacon had hired unimportant people to lend him their names for his great fraud. This was largely necessary because much of the work was treasonable at the time, and in his position as Chancellor he could not be associated with treason.

Many cryptographers studied Mrs. Gallup's work and criticized her methods of analysis. Much of this criticism was valid, but Bacon supporters refused to accept it. Mrs. Gallup finally admitted that she had used "inspiration" to distinguish between the two faces of type which, she claimed, existed in the original printing of Shakespeare's plays.

The Baconians by now were on the warpath. The next to bring out a book was a scholar and amateur cryptographer, William Booth. In his *Some Acrostic Signatures of Francis Bacon*, he discovered an elaborate system of acrostics carrying Bacon's name. An acrostic is a text, usually in verse, in which a set or several sets of letters, as the first, second or last letter of a line, when read in order, form a word, phrase or sentence.

For instance, Booth found three significant lines in Act IV, Sc. III of *Love's Labour's Lost*, which read:

> *But with the motion of all elements,*
> *Courses as swift as thought in every power,*
> *And gives to every power a double power.*

From these lines, Booth deduced this:

B
C O
A N

These letters he read as BACON.

Booth's "proofs" were not convincing and were soon discarded. But the Baconians were not finished yet. Colonel George Fabyan, of the American Army, was the next traveller along the road. But Colonel Fabyan differed from his predecessors; he was an able cryptographer. Discarding the Shakespeare Folio, he pinned his faith on Shakespeare's grave at Stratford.

The present inscription dates only from 1831, but copies of the original are in existence and it was the original Colonel Fabyan analyzed. Here is the present inscription:

GOOD FREND FOR IESVS SAKE FORBEARE
TO DIGG THE DVST ENCLOASED HEARE
BLESE BE Y MAN Y SPARES THES STONES
AND CVRST BE HE Y MOVES MY BONES

Shakespeare's Gravestone

The original inscription was made up partly of capitals, partly small letters, partly of three letters formed into one to make up the word "the." Fabyan claimed that here were three alphabets, making up a trilateral cipher. The first record of a trilateral cipher was in 1685, long after Bacon's death, but, as the colonel pointed out, many a cipher had been in use for a long time before its use was described in print.

Fabyan ingeniously analyzed the inscription to read: *Fr. Bacon hazards one ciph'r in a ms within WMR*. Fabyan did not explain what WMR could mean. But there are some serious objections to the Fabyan theory — as even he, being a competent cryptographer, would admit. The Baconian theory may be true, but as yet there is no conclusive cryptographic evidence to support it. But for

many years to come, cryptanalysts will be studying the
folio and the tombstone inscription. Perhaps one day the
grave will be opened and we will know if a manuscript
does lie hidden inside.

Let us take a quotation, as many a Baconian theorist
has done, and prove that Bacon wrote it. The quotation is
SILENCE IS THE VIRTUE OF FOOLS. If Bacon had wanted to
print this and enclose a secret message in it, he would ask
the typesetter to use two different faces, just as we have
done here:

SILENCE IS THE VIRTUE OF FOOLS.

To decipher this, we first break up the sentence into five-
letter groups:

SILEN CEIST HEVIR TUEOF FOOLS

Underneath each letter in light type, we put an **A** and
under each letter in bold type, a **B**.

	SILEN	**CEIST**	**HEVIR**	**TUEOF**	**FOOLS**
	AAAAB	AAAAA	AAABA	ABBAB	ABBAA
Standing for	B	A	C	O	N

Standing for
(refer to the
Bacon cipher)

The interesting thing about this is that Bacon *did* write
the sentence! Perhaps there could be more in the Baconian theory than most people will admit.

5

- **Cipher and Mary Queen of Scots**
- **Shorthand**
- **Brilliant Frenchmen**
- **The Downfall of Monarchs**
- **The Codes of Louis XIV**

COMPARED with countries like France and Italy, England early neglected cryptography, but during the reign of Elizabeth I, there were so many intrigues and plots that ciphers were bound to come into use. It was dangerous in those dramatic days to put anything on paper in straightforward English — and sometimes it was dangerous to encipher a message. It was not only dangerous for Mary Queen of Scots, but fatal; cipher sent her to the execution block.

One of the great cipher experts of the time was Sir Francis Walsingham, Elizabeth's Secretary of State. Walsingham first encountered cipher when he was travelling in Italy, after leaving Oxford. In Rome, he came across a copy of Jeronimo Cardano's book, and his alert brain saw instantly that cipher could be a weapon in state affairs. He studied Cardano's system and every other ref-

erence he could find on the subject. When, later, he was
appointed to his high position, he founded an Intelligence Service, to which he introduced cipher.

So seriously did Walsingham take cipher that he opened
a secret cipher school in London. All his agents took a
course in cryptography before they were entrusted with
service abroad. Walsingham had fifty-three spies on the
Continent, a large number in those days. One of Walsingham's star pupils, both as an agent and as a cryptographer, was Gilbert Gifford. Gifford was in prison when
he first made contact with Walsingham. "I have heard of
the work you do and I want to serve you," he wrote to
the Secretary of State. "I have no scruples and no fear of
danger. Whatever you order me to do I shall accom-
plish."

The moment he finished his prison sentence, Gifford
found himself in Walsingham's service. He was trained
in cipher work and then sent to spy on Mary Queen of
Scots, who was living at Fotheringay, England, in semi-
imprisonment. Mary was the great hope for many English and Scottish Catholics, who claimed that the English
throne was rightfully hers — she was, in fact, heir-ap-
parent — and that Elizabeth was a usurper. These people
wanted Elizabeth out of the way and Mary, Walsingham
believed, was involved in plots against her. It was Gifford's task to find proof.

True to his nature and his training, Gifford made contact with members of Mary's staff and posed as an ar-
dent Catholic ready to die for Mary. Before long, he was
presented to Mary, who had need of champions. Because

Gifford was a gifted actor, he became Mary's personal messenger.

One message Gifford was told to deliver was addressed to Thomas Babington, who was plotting with the King of Spain to depose Elizabeth and put Mary in her place. Gifford opened the package, found the message was in cipher and made a copy of it before he resealed the communication. The copy went to Walsingham, who worked over the cipher for only a few hours before he found the key.

This was damning evidence against Mary, but Walsingham wanted more. He sent Gifford back to intercept and copy more secret messages, which, before long, resulted in the arrest of all the conspirators, including Mary herself. In her apartments, the keys to about fifty ciphers were found, although they might well have been planted there by Walsingham's agents, as Mary's supporters claimed.

One message explained in detail an ingenious plot to kill Elizabeth, her great minister, William Cecil (Lord Burleigh) and Walsingham himself. Six men of Elizabeth's own household were supposed to be members of the conspiracy.

Shorthand was a form of secret writing in Elizabethan days. Stenography or tachygraphy was first used in 195 A.D. Certain types of shorthand were used by the Church right up to the 11th century.

Then, for several centuries, the art seemed to stagnate until Timothy Bright, an English doctor, published, in 1588, his *The Arte of Shorte, Swifte and Secrete Writ-*

ing. It was with Bright's book that shorthand, as we know it, had its beginning.

A	ǀ	H	⁊	P	⁊	Q	—o
B	˥	IJ	ʃ	R	℮		
C	ʃ	K	˥	S	⁊		
D	ˀ	L	ʔ	T	℮		
E	ʌ	M	৭	UVW	Q		
F	⁊	N	⁊	X	ɣ		
G	˥	O	⌐	Z	ɤ		

Bright's Shorthand Alphabet

Actually, in use, the system was not rapid; the student had to learn six hundred different characters and many words were expressed by only their two initial letters.

After Bright, several men evolved systems of "short and secret writing," until Isaac Pitman invented his famous "Phonographic" method, which was to spread across the world.

At the end of the 16th century, when the Spanish Empire covered much of the known world, Spanish agents communicated with each other and with their chiefs by means of a cipher system of more than five hundred signs. Some Spanish messages were captured by the French and were sent to the King, Henry IV, who promptly or-

dered his cipher expert, François Viète, a French mathe-
matician, to break the cipher. Viète managed to do so
and for two years the French were able to follow all
Spanish moves.

When the Spaniards found out that their cipher had
been broken, they were so furious they applied to the
Pope to have Viète tried before a Cardinals' Court as an
"archfiend in league with the devil." The Court sat, but
the Pope and his cardinals had more sense of humor
than the irate Spaniards, and Viète was never called to
give evidence. From our point of view, this is unfortunate, for Viète might have given history some interesting information.

Viète was not the only French expert. In French, there
is a word, *rossignol*, meaning an implement for opening
a lock when the key has been lost. It is a form of tribute
to the man who once owned the word as his name, M.
Antoine Rossignol, one of the great cryptographers of
history. It was he who made French cryptography su-
preme for many years.

Rossignol became a professional cryptographer by
chance. A keen amateur, he was sent for one day, in
1626, by the celebrated soldier, the Prince of Condé, to
break a secret message just captured after being sent
out of the besieged city of Réalmont, held by the Hugue-
nots.

The quiet, studious Rossignol, aged thirty-six, arrived at
Condé's headquarters, spent the day working on the mes-
sage, and before nightfall handed the solution to the
Prince. We know nothing more about the cipher other than

that it was in verse, but we do know its import. The commander of Réalmont was writing to a Huguenot force, saying that unless he received ammunition he could not hold out.

Condé, who previously had no idea of this state of affairs, sent the original message and the decipherment back to the city under flag of truce. Réalmont surrendered practically instantly.

The following year, 1627, the Huguenot fortress of La Rochelle was also under siege and messages both to and from the garrison had been captured. The great Cardinal Richelieu sent for Rossignol to decipher them. Rossignol did so with such ease that Richelieu set him up as head of a new department of secret writing. It was an historic decision for France, but even Richelieu did not realize what a genius Rossignol was.

As Louis XIII died, he told his queen that, above all other men in France, Rossignol must be protected and encouraged. Richelieu's successor, Cardinal Mazarin, was Rossignol's chief during the early years of Louis XIV's reign. When Mazarin died, Rossignol continued under the supervision of the monarch himself. From the time that he broke the Réalmont cipher, Rossignol served France for forty-seven years and was never once involved in any sordid intrigue.

Unfortunately, history does not know much about how Rossignol broke ciphers. He created ciphers, too, and, knowing the weakness of those in current use, he invented one that was indecipherable. In fact, this cipher, known as the Great Cipher of Louis XIV, remained indecipherable for more than two hundred years. When Rossignol died, the key was lost and, though experts worked on remaining messages for centuries, none succeeded in breaking it. It was a great tribute to Rossignol.

The interesting period of codes also began during the reign of Louis XIV, when codes were noted for their intricate design and ornamentation. Even color played a part in French codes of this period. France was full of plotters and intriguers, both French and foreign, and every visitor to France was issued with what amounted to a passport — one which told much more about the holder than does today's passport.

To begin with, there was a separate color for each nationality. An Englishman had a yellow paper; a Dutchman a white one, a Russian a white-green one. The paper held a lot of hidden information. Suppose, in the year 1650, a titled Englishman, Lord John Hope, arrived in Paris with letters of introduction to Count de Fareuil. The Count would not see his Lordship immediately, but would send his own secretary to bring back Lord John's identity paper.

He would scrutinize it carefully. The yellow paper was oval-shaped; therefore, Lord John was aged between twenty-five and thirty-five. Under his name were two small, thick strokes, indicating that Lord John was short and fat. In the corner of the paper was a rose, showing that the owner had a genial personality. Threaded through holes on the paper was a ribbon, which told Count de Fareuil that Lord John was a bachelor. He was rich; this much was shown by the particular design around the paper.

Again, a comma after Lord John's name indicated that he was a Protestant. Other punctuation on an identity paper revealed if the bearer was of another religion.

Apart from all this, the identity paper would tell if the bearer was a fool or acutely intelligent; if he was untrustworthy or highly reliable; if he was stubborn or easily convinced. And much more.

Another monarch who used ciphers was Charles I, and, as in the case of Mary, they were fatal. The charges brought against him were based on deciphered correspondence. Some historians go so far as to say that Charles was beheaded because of letters plotting against Parliament, written in cipher to his wife. During the English Civil War, the Parliamentary troops captured the letters at the Battle of Naseby, 1645, and Dr. John Wallis deciphered them.

6

- **The Escape of Sir John Trevanion**
- **Charles II's Cipher**
- **An Error in Cipher Makes a King**
- **Diplomatic Double Talk**

SIR John Trevanion, a Royalist who fought for the King, was more fortunate than his monarch, for a cipher message saved his life. He was captured by Cromwell's Roundheads and imprisoned in Colchester Castle. He did not expect to leave the place alive, for other prominent Royalists had been executed there. Probably, he used the simple Quadrilateral Alphabet to communicate with other prisoners. Used by prisoners for centuries, the Quadrilateral Alphabet consists of five groups of five letters, with Z omitted. The prisoner simply taps on the wall or on a pipe to attract the attention of his fellow-captive. Four taps followed by three taps stands for Group 4, third letter — namely, R. This method of cipher-signalling is slow, but then prisoners have plenty of time. There have been cases on record where a prisoner, when released, could give complete and accurate details of somebody "inside" with him — without ever having seen his face or having exchanged

a single word. He gained all his information by the Quadrilateral Alphabet.

While he waited for death, Sir John received a letter
from a friend, known only to history as "R.T."

Worthie Sir John: — Hope, that is ye beste comfort of
ye afflicted, cannot much, I fear me, help you now. That
I would say to you, is this only: if ever I may be able
to requite that I do owe you, stand not upon asking me.
'tis not much that I can do: but what I can do, bee ye
verie sure I wille. I knowe that, if dethe comes, if ordinary men fear it, it frights not you, accounting it for a
high honour, to have such a rewarde of your loyalty.
Pray yet that you may be spared this soe bitter, cup. I
fear not that you will grudge any sufferings; only if
bie submission you can turn them away, 'tis the part of
a wise man. Tell me, an if you can, to do for you any-
thinge that you wolde have dòne. The general goes back
on Wednesday. Restinge your servant to command. —
R. T.

A simple cipher message is contained in this letter and
Sir John Trevanion, who did not panic, was astute enough
to see it and to profit by it. The third letter after each
punctuation mark spells out this message: PANEL AT EAST
END OF CHAPEL SLIDES.

Sir John asked permission to spend an hour "privately
repenting" in the chapel. Actually, he spent the hour privately escaping, and because he managed to stay free we
know his story.

While exiled in Holland, Charles II, son of Charles I, had an elaborate cipher, probably created for him by Rossignol, through Louis XIV's orders. It was a syllabic numerical cipher. For instance, the syllable AB was represented by 70 and AC by 72. The numbers were disarranged, of course, and this was the cipher's greatest handicap — a lot of time was needed to both encipher and decipher a message. Still, time was one thing Charles II had plenty of at this period.

The scheme by James, Duke of Monmouth, and the Duke of Argyll to rebel and seize the throne from King James, in 1685, was upset because of cipher messages sent by Argyll to his followers in Scotland. The ciphers fell into the Government's hands, were broken and Monmouth and Argyll were really beaten before they started. They were both beheaded — victims of an inefficient cipher.

Few people realize today that the famous *Diary* of Samuel Pepys was written entirely in cipher. An Oxford University scholar, named John Smith, worked on it for three years before he broke it and transcribed it. He must have been exasperated when, much later, a complete key to the diary was found.

It should go without saying that the person sending a cipher message should see that it is accurate and legible. A single error can involve the decipherer in a lot of time, and wasted time can be dangerous. But if errors can be troublesome, they can also be beneficial, as Frederick, Elector of Brandenberg, found out at the beginning of the 18th century.

Frederick had only a duchy, but he was ambitious and

wanted to convert it into a kingdom. To do so, Frederick needed the consent of the Emperor of Austria and of the Holy Roman Empire. But Frederick was dubious about approaching this awe-inspiring ruler, who was noted for his unpredictable temper.

Frederick maintained a daily correspondence with his minister in Vienna, asking him to report at once when he saw a favorable moment to approach the Emperor. Both men used cipher and, to make their messages even safer, they referred to various people by numbers. Frederick himself was No. 24, the Emperor was No. 110 and an insignificant Jesuit priest, Father Wolf, was No. 116.

Frederick finally received what he was waiting for — a message from his minister giving him the go-ahead. "The time is favorable," the message said in effect, "and you should communicate with No. 110." *Or was it 116?* Frederick was unable to decide and was too impatient to write back and have the figure checked. He wrote a long and weighty letter to No. 116 — Father Wolf.

The Jesuit was astounded to receive the Royal application, but was extremely proud that Frederick should ask his help in the important matter of converting the Duchy of Prussia into a kingdom. Overcome by the implied compliment to both the Church and to himself, he forwarded Frederick's letter to the head of the Jesuit Order, together with a warm recommendation of his own. "Such a prince merits reward," Father Wolf wrote, "he proves his piety by asking the help of the Church. I am pleased and impressed by this approach."

The chief Jesuit was impressed, too. Through devious

channels, the all-powerful Church presented Frederick's
wish to the Emperor, who had no alternative but to agree,
no matter what he personally thought about the matter.
Prussia became a kingdom and Frederick a king. But had
he written to No. 110 — as his minister intended him to do
— he might forever have remained a prince.

Frederick II of Prussia had cipher trouble of a different
kind. Count Brühl, Prime Minister of Augustus III, Elector
of Saxony, organized a deciphering bureau — the Black
Chamber — at Dresden. All the messages sent by the King
of Prussia's ambassador in Dresden were opened, copied
and deciphered for a period of sixteen years — 1736-52.
As soon as the courier from Berlin arrived on Saxon territory at Grossenhayn, his bag was picked during the
change of horses. The official letters were abstracted and
sent by swift rider to Dresden, where the Black Chamber
unsealed, copied, resealed and returned them to the post,
without anybody being any the wiser. Saxony was constantly aware of the plans of Frederick II and, when necessary, reported them to Austria and Russia.

Double talk or code-jargon had been used in diplomatic
circles for centuries. In the mid-18th century, French envoys were issued with a small but elaborate code dictionary, in which nations, plots and armies were described in
terms of trade and invididuals under the names of furs.
This system was plausible only because the French Ambassador to Russia, for instance, had a real fur merchant on
his staff. When the Ambassador wanted to send a message, he would do so in ordinary language and deliberately
write into it various bits of misinformation for the benefit

of those people who would spy on it. His fur merchant would send another message to a colleague in Paris.

Fox is going out of fashion here and bear is gaining ground. I understand that Herr Bauder in Berlin counted on the arrival of a large quantity of moleskin, but this has probably been cancelled because the price was too high. The demand for wolf remains steady and we should, if necessary, be ready to trade with Herr Spiltz of Vienna.

The Paris furrier would take this message to his official contact who would refer it to the French Foreign Ministry, where officials would decode it as, roughly: England (fox) is unpopular, while Sweden (bear) is well regarded. Prussia had hoped for British military support (moleskins = British troops) but England wanted too much for them. Austria (wolf) is holding her ground and France should remain friendly with the Austrian Government.

This type of code had two weaknesses; a message could easily be misinterpreted and, if it did fall into the wrong hands, a single intelligent brain could fathom its hidden meaning. Its great advantage was that, generally, it concealed the existence of any secret message, and would get through readily.

The French were certainly aware that the British Secret Service was using codes. At one time, the Ministry of Police sent Napoleon a confidential report that French spies had learned that the British had borrowed words relating to music and botany for a jargon-code. Another report, still in existence, said that the British agents had been instructed to abandon music and botany and to switch to words connected with watchmaking, catering and cooking.

The French probably invented the idea of a code book and men of other nations gradually realized that this was an efficient system.

7

• The Man in the Iron Mask

ONE of the most famous prisoners in history was the "Man in the Iron Mask." His story is no longer a mystery, for the discovery and solution of a ciphered letter cleared it up conclusively. But, though the solution was discovered in 1893, many people still refer to the "mystery" of the "Man in the Iron Mask."

The mystery first arose when a prisoner was received in the prison of the fortress town of Pignerole in the Savoy, then French territory, now part of Italy. The citizens of the town saw him frequently as he walked on the battlements; they saw, too, that he had a soldierly bearing. But his features they could not see — for his face was always covered by a mask. The mask was probably not of iron. Only one contemporary described the mask as of iron, and this man's evidence is suspect. The mask was certainly black and probably it was of velvet.

It was said in Pignerole that the captive was an aristocrat. Guards passed the word that he often dined with the governor of the prison and treated him as an inferior. The guards had orders always to treat the prisoner with great respect.

All this gave rise to the rumors that the man must be of royal blood. Only one person in Pignerole had even the slightest chance to find out. This man, a leatherworker, was walking near the prison walls one day when the masked prisoner threw down to him a silver plate, on which various marks had been scratched.

The leatherworker was looking at the plate when guards rushed from the prison and dragged him inside. He spent weeks in a cold cell before the authorities were convinced of the truth of his claim that he could neither read nor write and that he was not involved in a plot to free the prisoner.

The captive was transferred to the Ile Sainte-Marguerite, another impregnable fortress, and finally he reached the grimmest prison of all, the Bastille, where, after thirty-one years in captivity, he died. But the mystery lived on.

Was he the twin brother of King Louis XIV? The son of Louis and his mistress Louise de la Vallière? The unwanted son of Anne of Austria? The mystery teased the imagination of men for many years.

Then, in 1890, Commandant Victor Gendron, while studying the campaigns of the French Marshal Catinat, came upon a ciphered letter. Gendron was no cryptographer, so he handed the letter to Commandant Bazières, a clever cipher expert in the French Army Cryptographic Department.

The cipher comprised groups of numbers, and Bazières found it remarkably difficult to break. In fact, he worked at it for three years before he solved it. It was one of the great cryptographic coups of history. The letter was signed by François de Louvois, Minister of War to Louis XIV, and it was addressed to Marshal Catinat.

What Commandant Bazières had broken down was nothing other than the Great Cipher of Louis XIV, undeciphered in centuries.

Versailles

To M. the Lieutenant-General de Catinat, Commander-in-Chief of the Army of Piedmont:

I have received the letters which you were good enough to send me on the first of the month.

I suppose it is unnecessary to tell you with what displeasure His Majesty receives the news of how flatly General Bulonde disobeyed his and your orders when he took it on himself to raise the siege of Coni. His Majesty knows better than any other person the consequences of this act, and he is also aware of how deeply our failure to take the place will prejudice our cause, a failure which must be repaired during the winter.

His Majesty desires that you immediately arrest General Bulonde and cause him to be conducted to the fortress of Pignerole, where he will be locked in a cell under guard at night, and permitted to walk the battlements during the day with a mask.

As the Governor of the fortress of Pignerole is under the orders of your military department, you will kindly give directions to him for the execution of His Majesty's desires.

I remain, sir, your most humble and obedient servant.

Louvois, Minister of War

Now the truth was known. The famous captive was Vivian Labbé, Seigneur de Bulonde, a lieutenant-general of the French Army. His cowardice and disobedience had sentenced him to a living death.

Coming from a man with Commandant Bazières' reputation, this decipherment was hailed as a great discovery and most people still accept it. One man who did not was an Englishman. He set out to prove that the Man in the Mask was James de la Cloche, illegitimate son of Charles II of England. He claimed that General Bulonde was alive two years after the death of the famous prisoner in the Bastille. The facts about Bulonde and his actions at Coni are historic truth, but I sometimes wonder why the decision to imprison him and to mask him had to be written in cipher.

8

- **An American Code Book**
- **Napoleon's Ciphers** • **Edgar Allan Poe**
- **Major Kasiski and His Importance**
- **Ciphers in the American Civil War**
- **The Transatlantic Cable Row** • **Morse Code**

IN 1776, Arthur Lee, an American, developed the idea of a code book. He used the system to correspond secretly with his brothers and later tried to interest Congress in it. His efforts must have had some success for, in 1789, the United States had an official code containing nearly 1,600 numbers, including one for every English syllable and many word signs, but it fell into disuse about 1815.

The book code still works efficiently today. Each person involved has a copy of some particular edition of a book, preferably a dictionary, because in it can be found any word required and without tedious search. The encipherer sends a series of numbers, giving the page and line on which may be found the word in question. The sender merely looks up his own copy of the dictionary and checks the numbers.

The system is reasonably safe, but probably would not work for international espionage. Any cryptographic department, worthy of the name, would have a copy of every dictionary printed and before long could break any code message. In fact, in 1918, the United States Army Cryptographic Department broke, within a few days, a dictionary code the Germans used to contact agents in South America.

While the United States was experimenting with code late in the 19th century, Napoleon Bonaparte had been making good use of ciphers. In fact, he was one of the first great soldiers to treat ciphers seriously and several of his marshals used them in the field. General Louis Suchet lost his to the Spaniards, who were able to break the General's messages to his garrisons. Using the information, they retook two fortresses from the French.

A French historian, General Charles Bardin, claims that the French campaigns of 1814 were disastrous because the Army lost nearly all its cipher officers during the retreat from Moscow in 1812. When Napoleon wanted to write to his distant garrisons, his Chief of Staff, Marshal Berthier, had to send orders in plain language, obviously a dangerous practice. Bardin wrote: "Perhaps the future of France and the map of Europe depended then on the use of cryptography."

During Napoleon's time, a M. Claude Chappé invented a series of high poles on which were movable arms, set up along the roads stretching from Paris to the distant French frontiers.

Each signal pole was visible from those on either side and each one had an operator. On its very first duty, the system carried the news of a victory from Strasbourg to Paris more than twelve hours before the fastest courier. The French were so pleased with the system that they took it with them into the countries of Eastern Europe.

One difficulty about the system was that anybody with a little observation and common sense could quickly learn to read these public messages; hence, ciphers became essential for state security. On top of this, during the 30's and 40's of the last century, much political intrigue was going on.

The lightning telegraph was one reason for the great revival of the use and popularity of cryptography, about the middle of the 19th century.

The American writer, Edgar Allan Poe, was attracted to cryptography and studied it avidly. In 1840, he published an article in which he claimed that no such thing as an unsolvable cipher existed. This was a rash statement, but Poe went further. He offered to solve all ciphers sent to him, though he took the precaution of specifying that they must be in English, of simple substitution type, and that the word divisions of the clear should be maintained; that is, they could not be formed into five-letter groups.

Hundreds of ciphered texts were sent to him and he broke them all. This was one of the more difficult, published in *Graham's Magazine* in 1840.

Ofoiiiiaso ortsiii sov eodisoioe afduiostifoi ft iftvi tri oistoiv oiniafetsorit ifeov rsri afotiiiiv rudiiot irio rivvio eovit atratfetsoria aioriti iitri tf oitovin tri aetifei ioreitit sov usttoi oioittstifo dfti afdooitior trso ifeov tri dfit otfteov softriedi ft oistoiv oriofiforiti suitteii viireiiiitifoi ft tri iarfoisiti iiti trir uet otiiiotiv uitfti rid io tri eoviiee-iiiv rfasueostr ft tri dftrit tfoeei . . .

The solution to this is:

Nonsensical phrases and unmeaning combinations of words, as the learned lexicographer would have confessed himself, when hidden under cryptographic ciphers, serve to perplex the curious enquirer and baffle penetration more completely than would the most profound apothegms of learned philosophers. Abstruse disquisitions of the scholiasts, were they but presented before him in the undisguised vocabulary of the mother tongue.

The cipher was keyed by a Latin phrase which took up all the clear:

A	B	C	D	E	F	G	H	I	J	K	L	M	N
S	U	A	V	I	T	E	R	I	N	M	O	D	O

O	P	Q	R	S	T	U	V	W	X	Y	Z
F	O	R	T	I	T	E	R	I	N	R	E

Even in possession of the key, you would probably have a lot of trouble in deciphering this message.

But nobody in the British War Office had any difficulty in deciphering a code message sent from India by General Sir Charles Napier. The message was PECCAVI — Latin for "I have sinned." It was one of the shortest and wittiest messages in code history, for Napier had just captured the Indian province of Sindh.

In 1863, a German army officer, Major Kasiski, published a major book on cryptography—the first important one in a century. Kasiski's system is today the basis of modern cryptography, especially in its serious aspects. Kasiski did more than suggest methods of encipherment; he explained how the Vigenère system could be broken. This was a milestone in the cryptographic art for, up to this time, the Vigenère system was believed to be unbreakable.

Kasiski's plan of decipherment was based on what should have been two obvious facts: *One*, in all languages, certain bigrams, trigrams and even longer groups of letters are frequently repeated. *Two*, it is practically impossible to write a message without repeating words. Kasiski and Edgar Allan Poe between them had a profound effect on cryptography, for they showed that at that time there was no unbreakable system. Louis XIV's Great Cipher was not broken until 1893.

During the American Civil War, the Union used a combination code-cipher which was much more successful than it should have been. It was a mere word transposition and simple to solve.

This is a message of the period:

To: *George C. Maynard, Washington, D.C.,*

Regulars ordered of my to public out suspending received 1862 spoiled thirty I dispatch command of continue of best otherwise worst Arabia my command discharge duty of last for Lincoln September period your from sense shall duties until Seward ability to the I a removal evening Adam herald tribute.

Philip Brunner

If I give you a few facts about this message, you should be able to solve it. The address and signature were "covers" and do not come into the decipherment. The word REGULARS was a code word, showing that the clear had been written in five columns of nine words each and giving the order in which the groups should be written down. These words were nulls: TRIBUNE, HERALD, SPOILED, SEWARD, FOR, WORST. LINCOLN was code for Louisville, Kentucky; ADAM a code for General Henry Wager Halleck; ARABIA code for General Buell. The word PERIOD simply indicates a full stop. The cipher was written by taking the columns in this order: Four, three, five, two, one, and then writing the words as in an ordinary letter.

If you cannot work out this simple transposition, this is what the columns looked like without the nulls:

	Lincoln September	*thirty*	1862	
Adam	period	I	received	last
evening	your	dispatch	suspending	my
removal	from	command	Out	of
a	sense	of	public	duty
I	shall	continue	to	discharge
the	duties	of	my	command
to	the	best	of	my
ability	until	otherwise	ordered.	Arabia.

As you can see, the message was enciphered by running up the fourth column, down the third, up the fifth, down the second and up the first. Yet this simple system completely baffled the Confederates.

The laying of the first transatlantic cable, in 1866, gave secret writing another push forward, and caused a row between the United States Secretary of State and the cable company. Secretary of State Henry Seward had to send an urgent message to Paris and it was vital that it remain secret, so the old 1789 diplomatic code was dug up and the message was transmitted in 1,100 groups of three, four or five figures. The message averted a war between the United States and France, but this was no comfort to Seward when he received the cable company's bill for $23,000. He protested strongly and was told that the company had been most reasonable; to a member of the public the cost would have been $92,000. The Government refused to pay the bill and it is still outstanding. The code was never again used.

The best-known code of all is Morse Code, although — as I have already said — it is not a code at all.

Samuel Morse was born in 1791 in Charlestown, Massachusetts.

After graduating from Yale University, Morse studied painting for a long time, but in 1832 he conceived the idea of electrical telegraphy, and this led to his famous code.

Everybody has seen Morse's code, which can be used not only in telegraphy but with whistle blasts, light flashes and even flags. He did not choose his symbols haphazardly but according to alphabetical frequency. For instance, the letter E was given the briefest symbol of all — a single dot.

This is his code:

A	•—	J	•———	S	•••
B	—•••	K	—•—	T	—
C	—•—•	L	•—••	U	••—
D	—••	M	——	V	•••—
E	•	N	—•	W	•——
F	••—•	O	———	X	—••—
G	——•	P	•——•	Y	—•——
H	••••	Q	——•—	Z	——••
I	••	R	•—•		

One great advantage of Morse's code is that it can be used in any language. It can also be learned rapidly. Most armies allow trainee signallers ten days to learn it thoroughly, but Morse himself always claimed that any intelligent person could learn it in an hour. Training is necessary for speed in sending and in receiving which, in fact, is the more difficult.

9

- **Army Ciphers**
- **Frustration for the Turks**
- **Success for the French — the St. Cyr Code**
- **The British Playfair Cipher**
- **Lord Wolseley's Square**
- **The Double Parallel Alphabet**

THE French were largely beaten by their own ciphers in the war with Germany in 1870-71. The French, besieged in Paris, sent messages to Army units in the country framed in such elementary cipher that the Germans had no difficulty in breaking the ciphers and blocking any French move. For much the same reason, the Russians beat the Turks in 1877.

The Turks had an unfortunate experience. The Ottoman Field-Marshal, Osman Pasha, entrusted one of his generals, Selim Pasha, with a confidential mission, Selim happened to be the chief cipher officer and, being a cautious man, he kept the code in his pocket. It was securely in his pocket when he went on·the mission. All the time he was away, ciphered telegrams and messages mounted up on the desk of Osman Pasha, but he was unable to read a single one and nobody on the staff was bright enough to break the cipher. He must have been one of the most frustrated generals in history.

The new speed and scale of war demanded rapid, accurate and secret communications. By 1880, cipher was no longer a military luxury, but a vital necessity, and every military power brought new brains and a lot of money to the subject.

The French came up with one of the best ideas — the St. Cyr Cipher — named after the famous military academy and shown below.

The St. Cyr Cipher

The top alphabet is stationary and is in normal order, with the letters spaced exactly the same distance apart. On the slide — which is movable — are two alphabets, both reversed in this case though this is not essential.

Suppose our key letter is P. We slide the lower alphabets along until P comes directly under A. Then all the cipher-equivalents to be used in enciphering are under the clear letter of the upper strip. To encipher the clear word RETREAT, we would write YLWYLPW.

This is one of the best and speediest ways of enciphering a message and it will defy analysis for as long as any other simple cipher.

It was one of the few which met the military essentials for secret communication — simplicity, rapidity, practicability, secrecy, accuracy, economy. The need for speed in a combat zone cannot be overemphasized. If information is to be of any use it must get through quickly; and to be enciphered and deciphered quickly, it must be simple. In any case, an enciphering clerk, working under great pressure and stress, is prone to make errors on a complicated cipher.

The British Army used code books early in the Boer War, but, when many had to be destroyed because of the danger of capture, the Army had to find a substitute. At first, officers communicated with one another in Latin, for the chances of the Boers being able to read Latin were remote. But then not all British officers knew Latin.

The British Army wanted a cipher with these qualities:

It had to be easily taught.

It had to baffle interceptors long enough for orders to be carried out without interference.

It must have no clumsy apparatus.

The answer to these requirements was the famous Playfair Cipher, one of the simplest and best substitution ciphers ever devised, and certainly the most outstanding of the period.

You can easily make it work for yourself. Find a key word and build up a five-line square, first writing the letters of the key word, and then the remaining letters of the alphabet in their correct sequence, leaving out those already contained in the key word. Also, omit J as I takes its place. We will assume that MASTER is the key word.

```
M   A   S   T   E
R   B   C   D   F
G   H   I   K   L
N   O   P   Q   U
V   W   X   Y   Z
```

The message we want to send is PATROL LEAVES AT DAWN. We break this up into letter groups, and if a word contains an unequal number of letters we add an x. Our message, broken up, reads:

PA TR OL LE AV ES AT DA WN.

We encipher the message in these groups. For instance, we take PA, find them on the Playfair square, and replace them with the two letters at the opposite corners of the diagonals they form. Hence, for PA we write SO, for TR put down MD and for OL we write HU.

There are a few exceptions to the diagonal rule. Where our two letters fall in the same line of the square, we encipher them by taking the letter immediately to the right of each, as in the case of ES (in LEAVES). So we write MT. If we have letters in the same column, as in the case of LE, we replace them by taking the letter that appears directly under each, UF. Our full message will read: SOMDHU FUMWRT SE TB OV. To make it appear more complicated, we could break up the message into three-letter groups: SOM DHU FUM WRT SET BOV.

The cipher can be made even more difficult to break

by arranging to make every third, fourth or fifth letter a dummy.

An enemy intercepting our sample message would find it difficult to solve without the key word. The person with the key word has no trouble. All he does is write out his square and reverse the original process. The first two letters, so, are at the corners of a diagonal, so he takes the opposite diagonal, in this case PA. And so on. With brief practice, it is possible to decipher a lengthy message in a few minutes.

The people in on the secret do not, of course, stick to the same key word. This would be foolish and dangerous. The word is changed to a prearranged timetable, perhaps twice daily or even hourly. Then, if after laborious work, an interceptor tracks down one key word, all his efforts will have been wasted.

This cipher has a few minor difficulties. If two letters appear in the same line and one of them is the final letter, we encipher it by taking the letter that would be to the right of it if it were moved into the initial place in the line. In our MASTER Playfair square, for instance, if we wanted to encipher SE, we would write T to begin with — then replace E with M. Where two letters are in the same column and the second one is at the foot of the column, we assume it to be at the top of the column and write down the letter beneath it. For instance, to encipher KY we write QT. For diagonals we take the shortest route. When the four letters form a square, the route is optional; this is the system's weakness.

Another interesting substitution cipher of the time was

Lord Wolseley's Square. Lord Garnet Joseph Wolseley was one of Britain's most famous generals and, late in the 18th century, he was Commander in Chief of the British Army. It is doubtful if he evolved the cipher which bears his name, but there is no doubt that he used it.

The system needs a key word, which is written down in the numbered squares, followed by the other letters of the alphabet, omitting J. Key word: PECULIAR.

1 P	2 E	3 C	4 U	5 L
8 I	9 A	10 R	11 B	6 D
7 F	12 G	H	12 K	7 M
6 N	11 O	10 Q	9 S	8 T
5 V	4 W	3 X	2 Y	1 Z

You will note that each number recurs twice and that the middle square is not numbered at all. One brief message sent by Lord Wolseley's Headquarters to the British Embassy in Cairo was: REINFORCEMENTS NEEDED.

To encipher this, we find R, the first letter, in its square, which is numbered 10. Now look at the second square numbered 10, and in it is the letter Q, which becomes our substitute for R. The E of our clear word is in square 2; the second number 2 square contains Y. And so on. The cipher message reads: QYTDMBQXYFYDIA DYYNYN.

The middle square does not have a number because it cannot be paired, so if we have a letter in our message corresponding to the letter in this square, we use the true letter in the cipher.

It is important to note that cipher messages are nearly always sent in groups of five letters or figures. There are two good reasons for this. It is easier for an operator to send a message in uniform groups and this form hides the number of letters in the words of the clear message.

One of the best and simplest substitution ciphers is the Double Parallel-Alphabet Cipher, also evolved from a key word. This is so quick and easy to use, it deserves to be popular with schoolboys and, in fact, it was the one I used at school when exchanging important secrets with my closest friends.

We write down the key word, which must have at least seven letters, followed by the remaining letters of the alphabet. Underneath this, we write the alphabet straight out. *Key word*: CIPHERS.

C	I	P	H	E	R	S	A	B	D	F	G	J
A	B	C	D	E	F	G	H	I	J	K	L	M

K	L	M	N	O	Q	T	U	V	W	X	Y	Z
N	O	P	Q	R	S	T	U	V	W	X	Y	Z

We want to send the message: STAY PUT.

Find s in the straight alphabet. It falls under Q, which becomes the cipher letter for s. The complete cipher will read: QTCY MUT. Several cipher letters are the same as in the clear but, if anything, this makes the message a little more difficult to break. As always, the key word should be changed frequently.

10

- **Transposition Ciphers**
- **Some More Substitutions**
- **The Two-step Cipher**

You saw an example of transposition cipher at the beginning of this book. It is merely one in which the letters remain the same as in the clear, but are shuffled to some specific pattern.

A simple but effective transposition cipher is the Chinese cipher, so-called because the message runs up and down the columns, Chinese style. Our message is: DANGEROUS TO REMAIN HERE. WE ARE LEAVING NOW.

This breaks into six columns of six words each. We begin with column six, writing down, go on to column five, writing up, and so on.

```
W   R   A   E   R   D
O   E   E   M   O   A
N   L   W   A   T   N
G   E   E   I   S   G
N   A   R   N   U   E
I   V   E   H   O   R
```

The cipher, in six-letter groups, would read:

WRAERD OEEMOA NLWATN GEEISG NARNUE IVEHOR.

An equally simple substitution cipher is the "Porta Simple," ideal for use with short messages. The Porta Simple, which is merely a shortened version of the Porta Table, uses four different alphabets.

Our clear message is: PLEASE SEND FUNDS URGENTLY. Giving each alphabet an identification letter, we construct them this way:

A	A	B	C	D	E	F	G	H	I	J	K	L	M
	N	O	P	Q	R	S	T	U	V	W	X	Y	Z
B	A	C	E	G	I	K	M	O	Q	S	U	W	Y
	B	D	F	H	J	L	N	P	R	T	V	X	Z
C	M	L	K	J	I	H	G	F	E	D	C	B	A
	Z	Y	X	W	V	U	T	S	R	Q	P	O	N
D	L	M	J	K	H	I	F	G	D	E	B	C	A
	N	O	P	Q	R	S	T	U	V	W	X	Y	Z

Cipher: A – CYRNFR B – TFMC C – SHAQF
D – GHUWLFNC.

All we have done is to write down each alphabet in a different way and to halve them. To encipher a letter, we merely take the opposite one in the other half. If the message were longer, we would simply start over again with A. I think the Porta system is worth showing again because it is one of the most useful ciphers.

One simple transposition is the Vertical Parallel. Suppose we want to send the brief statement RENDEZVOUS ON SATURDAY. We write down the words in this way:

R   O
E   N
N   S
D   A
E   T
Z   U
V   R
O   D
U   A
S   Y

The cipher is created by writing down each pair of letters RO EN NS DA ET ZU VR OD UA SY. Then, in the usual practice, the message is prepared for sending in five-letter groups:

ROENN   SDAET   ZUVRO   DUASY

The intended recipient of the message merely reverses the process, according to the prearranged plan.

The Double Transposition Cipher is a development of the simple transposition. It looks very complicated when written, but it is quite simple to prepare. Suppose our message is:

WE NEED DEFINITE INSTRUCTIONS BEFORE

PROCEEDING FURTHER.

This message contains forty-nine letters which are easily written out in seven columns.

	1	2	3	4	5	6	7
1	W	E	N	E	E	D	D
2	E	F	I	N	I	T	E
3	I	N	S	T	R	U	C
4	T	I	O	N	S	B	E
5	F	O	R	E	P	R	O
6	C	E	E	D	I	N	G
7	F	U	R	T	H	E	R

We have previously arranged with the recipient of our messages that we will shuffle the columns in a certain sequence, in this case 6325471. This means that column 6 becomes column 1, column 3 becomes column 2, and so on, resulting in this change:

	6	3	2	5	4	7	1
1	D	N	E	E	E	D	W
2	T	I	F	I	N	E	E
3	U	S	N	R	T	C	I
4	B	O	I	S	N	E	T
5	R	R	O	P	E	O	F
6	N	E	E	I	D	G	C
7	E	R	U	H	T	R	F

We have now made one transposition, by changing the letters across the page. Now we make the double transposition by changing the letters downward, using the same cipher numbering.

	6	3	2	5	4	7	1
6	N	E	E	I	D	G	C
3	U	S	N	R	T	C	I
2	T	I	F	I	N	E	E
5	R	R	O	P	E	O	F
4	B	O	I	S	N	E	T
7	E	R	U	H	T	R	F
1	D	N	E	E	E	D	W

You might think that by painstaking trial and error an expert could fairly quickly convert this cipher to its original order — and so he could. This is why we now set out the cryptogram in our routine five-letter groups, reading thus: NEEID GCUSN RTCIT IFINE ERROP EOFBO ISNET ERUHT RFDNE EEDWX.

The intended recipient simply reverses the enciphering process according to the arrangement made previously. It is surprising how quickly this can be done.

One numerical substitution device that offers four variations for each letter is interesting and can give an analyst a lot of trouble to break.

First of all, we write down the clear alphabet (omitting J) horizontally and a four-letter key word vertically.

```
      A B C D E F G H I K L M N
C
L
U
E


      O P Q R S T U V W X Y Z
C
L
U
E
```

We use 100 numbers, in pairs, from 00 to 99, and divide them into four groups, 00-24; 25-49; 50-74; 75-99. Each group is written down from left to right, according to the key word. That is, the first group begins under the letter c, the second group under l, the third under u, and the last group under e. (See illustration on next page.)

The advantage of this system is that it gives many different combinations for writing a word. For example, the word "the" can be enciphered sixty-four different ways, beginning with 16-05-02. With a little practice, a cryptographer could encipher even a lengthy message quickly.

To make a cipher really difficult for anybody not supposed to be in possession of it, we can indulge in the Two-Step Cipher, in which the message, usually enciphered by simple or double substitution, is then enciphered a second time. The second substitution is generally made from a set table, of which both sender and recipient must have copies.

	A	B	C	D	E	F	G	H	I	K	L	M	N	O	P	Q	R	S	T	U	V	W	X	Y	Z
C	23	24	00	01	02	03	04	05	06	07	08	09	10	11	12	13	14	15	16	17	18	19	20	21	22
L	40	41	42	43	44	45	46	47	48	49	25	26	27	28	29	30	31	32	33	34	35	36	37	38	39
U	56	57	58	59	60	61	62	63	64	65	66	67	68	69	70	71	72	78	74	50	51	52	53	54	55
E	96	97	98	99	75	76	77	78	79	80	81	82	83	84	85	86	87	88	89	90	91	92	93	94	95

Suppose we want to send NEED CASH. First, we encipher the clear by using the Double Parallel-Alphabet Cipher, with the key word CRUSOE.

C	R	U	S	O	E	A	B	D	F	G	H	I
A	B	C	D	E	F	G	H	I	J	K	L	M

J	K	L	M	N	P	Q	T	V	W	X	Y	Z
N	O	P	Q	R	S	T	U	V	W	X	Y	Z

Enciphered message: JOOS UCPB.

By referring to our table, which gives numerical values for each pair of letters, we find that JO = 101; OS = 316; UC = 54; PB = 777. We finally send the message 101 316 54 777. The numerical table could be a lengthy one and might fill many pages, so no secret agent would use this method.

Another useful two-step technique is the Combination Cipher, in which a message is first enciphered by transposition and then by substitution.

As before, we encipher NEED CASH to its substitute of JOOS UCPB, which, according to our prearrangement, is now written down:

J O   U P

    O S   C B

Finally, we send the message as JOUP OSCB. Deciphering is no problem to anybody in the know, but would be difficult for a stranger.

11

- **Dots, Lines, Zigzags and Triangles**
- **The Cipher Clock and Cipher Machine**
- **Symbol Codes**

INTERESTING and effective ciphers can be formed by dots, lines, zigzags and triangles. No words at all are used, so the ciphers can be pinpricks on a page, threads on a piece of cloth or designs on a drawing. All that the sender and recipient need is the alphabet key.

All these systems can be illustrated together, using, for the sake of simplicity, the alphabet in clear.

To decipher these messages, read from left to right, starting with the highest symbol. Each dot stands for a letter. Each end of every line and each change of direction indicates a letter. The message is the same in all illustrations — STAND FIRM.

All these ciphers can be made more difficult to break by changing the order of the alphabet. Provided each person in on the secret has a copy of the alphabet with the prearranged spacing, it does not matter in what sequence the letters appear.

Of course, if a message is long enough, all these ciphers can be readily broken by observing the frequency of the position of any dot, line or angle.

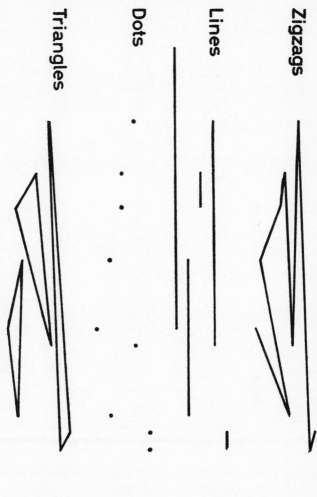

Zigzags

Lines

Dots

Triangles

Zigzags, Lines, Dots and Triangles

A B C D E F G H I J K L M N O P Q R S T U V W X Y Z

People who need ciphers today use some very complex instruments to enable them to encipher a long message quickly. Most of them are based on the simple Cipher Clock, which anybody can make with two paper or cardboard circles, one smaller than the other. Around the edge of each, print the straight alphabet, then pin the circles together so that the smaller can revolve. You also need a pointer which can move. Finally, we want a key word, say, UNCLE. Our message is SEND ANOTHER AGENT NOW.

We set this out as before:

Key word:
U N C L E U N C L E U N C L E U N C L
S E N D A N O T H E R A G E N T N O W

The first letter of the key word is U. With the clock, we find U on the outer circle; now we choose any letter on the inner circle to tally with U. This is our key letter and we will choose Z. Now we turn the inner circle until Z is opposite U, and set the pointer on these letters.

To begin enciphering, pick out every letter of the clear over which the U of the clear word appears. They are S, N, R, T. Find these letters on the outer circle and note down their opposite letters on the inner circle — B, G, C, A.

We can now begin to write down our message:

Key word:
U N C L E U N C L E U N C L E U N C L
Message:
S E N D A N O T H E R A G E N T N O W
Cipher:
B   G   C   A

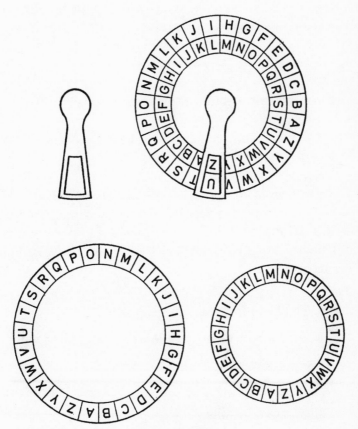

Cipher Clock

Now set the pointer so that the second letter of the key word, N, is opposite the key letter, Z. The letters of the message coming under N are E, O, A and N and we replace them as before: I, Y, M and Z. Fill in these letters on the cipher message:

BI   GY   CM   AZ

If you complete the cipher message, you will see how it is done.

To decipher a Cipher Clock message you will, of course, know the key word and key letter and simply reverse the process.

Symbol codes are still in use. Road signs and Boy Scout signs are codes of a type, even though they are meant to convey information and not to conceal it. The fraternity of tramps has its own particular collection of signs. For instance:

⊕ The people here will give you food.

▢ Stay away, these people will want you to work.

〰 Savage dog here.

🈐 By adopting a threatening attitude you might get results.

⌣ A hard-luck story goes down here.

⚇ Women only in this place.

○ ○ ○ Money here.

Not that these signs are new. They have been traced back to the 15th century, when the *Mordbrenner* — gangs of wandering criminals — used them throughout Central Europe.

Knowledge of criminals' signs enabled the great German criminologist, Professor Hans Gross, to warn police of an intended crime, some years ago. On the wall of a church in Austria, Gross saw this drawing — technically an ideograph.

Criminals' Sign Writing

He studied it, then told the local police that they should set a trap for two or more criminals who would be meeting near the church on Christmas Day. They would be planning a major theft. Sure enough, the men were caught and found to be robbers with long records and plans to commit a crime.

Gross explained the meaning of the sketch. The parrot,

drawn with a single line, stood for the underworld name of a crook known as "the Parrot." The church was self-explanatory, while the key meant that the church was the place to be robbed. The drawing below it was intended to be a baby, a symbol representing Christmas Day. The three stones stood for St. Stephen, who was stoned to death.

"It was quite simple," Gross said. "The Parrot wanted to rob the church on December 26, St. Stephen's Day. But he needed somebody to help him and anybody willing to do so should meet him at the church on Christmas Day to plan the theft."

12

- **Colonel Redl Betrays His Country**
- **The "Honorable" Seller of Codes**
- **Austrian Success**
- **General Hindenburg's Victory at the Battle of Tannenburg**
- **The Russians Capture a Code**
- **Room 40 of the Admiralty**
- **The Zimmerman Telegram**
- **German Ciphers**

So many codes and ciphers were invented late in the last century that, by 1900, every nation was obsessed with the idea of secret writing. Sensational fiction stories have been written about stolen codes, but probably truth in this case is much stranger than fiction. Between 1900 and 1914, every nation in Europe was trying to steal the codes of other nations. Most of the intrigue went on in Vienna, for it was here that international plots took place. It was from Vienna that the highly trusted, brilliant Austrian, Colonel Alfred Redl, betrayed to the Russians every military secret his country owned. His wholesale treachery was largely responsible for the catastrophic defeats suffered by the Austrians in the early days of World War I.

Then came the theft of the enormous Austrian master-code book from its safe in Vienna. In this book was kept the key to many communications. A Russian officer kindly told the Austrians who had stolen it — an Italian countess who hoped to make a lot of money from its sale. The Russian did not mention that his country already had a copy of the book, sold to them by Colonel Redl.

The long-suffering Austrians were also caught by a man, supposed to be a Balkan count, who offered to sell them a copy of the Serbian diplomatic code. The Austrian officer he dealt with was not altogether a fool and he demanded proof that the code was genuine. "Keep the book for a few days' free trial," the Serb offered generously. "I am an honorable man."

During the next few days, two diplomatic telegrams arrived addressed to the Serbian Ambassador in Vienna. Copies were sent from the Post Office and, sure enough, they were readily decoded by use of the book. The count called back and the Austrian officials paid him 10,000 kronen, after which he disappeared.

Five days later, another message in code arrived for the Serbian Ambassador and, eagerly, the Austrians deciphered their copy of it: THE MALE MOTHER OF THE WARSHIP HAS BEEN BUILT, the message said. Obviously, there had been a mistake somewhere. Using the code book they had bought, the startled Austrians made up a message in the code and had an agent in Belgrade send it to the Serbian Ambassador in Vienna, marked URGENT.

Less than an hour later, a Serbian Embassy official arrived at the Vienna Post Office with three messages. "These have arrived in an impossibly confused condition," he complained. "I want them repeated."

The three messages comprised the two sent by the "Count" and the one sent by the Belgrade agent. The Austrians knew then that they had been foiled. They had bought an elaborate fake code. The two messages decoded with the book had been sent by an accomplice of the "Count." The Serbian Ambassador, as the trickster well knew, was a lazy, incompetent man and he had not bothered to have the messages decoded at once.

Still, the Austrians had a big success, too. One observant cryptographer — and keen observation is a major part of a cryptographer's equipment — noticed that in ordinary straightforward messages in clear, the envoys of most nationalities used a standard opening pattern. For example, the English Ambassador invariably began, "I have the honor to inform you . . ." Was it possible, the cryptographer wondered, that code messages began in a conventional way?

A check showed that they did and, in quite a short time, the Austrians broke the diplomatic code of every nation represented in Austria. By 1914, Austria had code books almost as complete as those possessed by the unsuspecting ambassadors.

The English, the French, the Italians and others all had a finger in the sticky cryptographical pie in the prewar years, and the full story of the intrigues would make fascinating reading. Unfortunately, it is buried deep in Government archives.

In August 1914, the Germans sent a famous radio code message to all embassies, ships and stations abroad to tell them of the declaration of war. It was: A SON IS BORN. It was a strange code for such a message, for the son was to become a monster which devoured whole nations.

Behind the scenes in any war, the cryptographers are busy. They have their successes and they have their failures, but neither has any publicity. One of the greatest cryptographic disasters in history happened to the Russian Armies in 1914.

The First Army and the Second Army, operating in Galicia, were cut off by road and rail and their only communication was by radio. A brand new cipher had just come into use in the Russian Army. The Russians had been very clever about this cipher. They knew that the Germans had broken all old Russian ciphers, but they went on using them, making sure that no really important information found its way into the ciphers. Then, realizing that war was imminent, the Russians had evolved the new cipher which was not to be put into use until war was declared. This, they correctly reasoned, would give them an initial advantage against Germany. But here, Russian Intelligence ended. There was only one copy of the cipher, owned by General Jilinsky, but he had given it to General Rennenkampf of the First Army. The First Army, therefore, sent its messages in this cipher — but the Second Army could not decipher them.

The Second Army reverted to the old cipher in an effort to establish communications, but the First Army, in obedience to General Jilinsky's orders, had already destroyed its keys. So the two great armies could not correspond and a chaotic situation developed. Both generals, in desperation, began to send message in clear. This was even more dangerous than not sending messages at all.

The enemy commander, General Paul von Hindenburg of the German Army, was worried because his force was much inferior to the Russians' and if the two enemy armies joined up, as he expected them to, he would be overwhelmed.

To his astonishment, his Intelligence reported that the two Russian commanders were exchanging messages in clear. At first, Hindenburg suspected that this was a ruse to trap him, but he soon realized that this was not so. One day, Hindenburg's Intelligence Officer rushed to him with a message just picked up from General Rennenkampf to Jilinsky. The message read, in effect: I AM HALTING TEMPORARILY AND CANNOT LINK WITH YOU AS MY SUPPLY TRAINS HAVE NOT ARRIVED.

Hindenburg was no longer worried. Relieved and confident, he attacked. The battle, known to history as the Battle of Tannenberg, was all over in three days, with the Russians completely defeated. It was one of the most decisive victories in history — and all because the Russians had not been competent cryptographers.

As some recompense for the humiliation of the Russian Army at Tannenberg, the Russian Navy scored over the Germans in the matter of some vital naval code books. In 1914, a German cruiser, the *Magdeburg*, after raiding Russian Baltic Sea ports, ran aground in a fog. Knowing that attack and capture were imminent, her captain ordered an officer to take the code books to deep water and sink them.

The officer was about to climb overboard into a rowboat when Russian warships opened fire, and an explosion blew him overboard. Later, when Russian seamen were picking German bodies from the water, they found this officer with the lead covers of the code books still clasped in his arms, but the books themselves had vanished. Divers went down into the shallow water and found them, still undamaged. They were rushed to the British Admiralty in London.

One of the most important parts of the Admiralty was Room 40, headquarters of the Royal Navy's cryptographic section, commanded by Admiral Sir Reginald Hall. These key men had been working on the German codes for some time but with strictly limited success until the *Magdeburg's* code books arrived.

Once Room 40 had mastered the codes, the German Navy had no chance. Time after time their ships were surprised by British squadrons. Before the Battle of Jutland, Room 40 knew the position of every German ship and actually radioed the informatiion to Admiral Jellicoe. Owing to atmospheric interference, the report did not reach the Admiral, though the Royal Navy was successful in any case.

It was a German code message that brought American opinion into favor of war in 1917. This was the occasion of the famous Zimmerman Telegram, when the German ambassador to Mexico was ordered to bring about an alliance with Japan to attack the United States, with the help of Mexico. Mexico was offered three American states for her trouble. This inflammatory telegram had been decoded, like so many before it, in Room 40.

The news was released by Admiral Hall. At the end of his interview with reporters, he said casually, "Wasn't it clever of the Americans to do just what we have been trying to do ever since the war started? They succeeded in breaking the original text of a German diplomatic telegram."

This little piece of play-acting deceived the Press of Britain, America and France but it did not fool the Germans. They knew that Admiral Hall had been covering up the work of British agents. In fact, Hall was protecting a man named Alexander Szek, a young Austrian working at the big radio station in Brussels, from which Germany sent messages all over the world. Szek, unknown to the Germans, had an English mother and was pro-English. For many months, Szek stole a few words each day from the German diplomatic code book. In the end, the British had all of it, but they told Szek to stay at his post, in case his leaving made the Germans suspicious.

They were certainly suspicious after the disclosure of the Zimmerman Telegram and concentrated their attention on the Brussels radio station. The British spirited Szek out of Brussels and across the Belgian border into France, but the courageous young Anglo-Austrian never did reach Britain. He vanished and was never heard of again. Some rumors said that he had been caught by the Germans, others that the British themselves "disposed" of Szek for reasons of security.

When the Germans changed their naval code after the
Battle of Jutland, the British got a copy of the new code
— by salvaging it from a sunken enemy submarine. They
went right on sending divers down to sunken submarines and, through the war years, managed to acquire
enough code books to keep up with German changes.
Later, when a German Zeppelin was shot down over
France, American soldiers salvaged a code chart showing the position and call sign of every German submarine
in service. The chart had been torn up but the pieces
were found and diligently fitted together. It was one of
the great code scoops of the war.

But the Germans had not been unsuccessful. They had
broken the British Playfair method and all ciphers and
most codes being used by the French and Russians. They
scored a shrewd hit against the Russian Navy in the Black
Sea. The Germans had only three warships in the Black
Sea and, being heavily outnumbered by the Russians,
they were unable to achieve very much. So, in Russian
naval code, the Germans sent the Russian admiral an order to take his entire fleet to Trebizond, at the eastern
end of the Black Sea. While the Russians steamed off on
this pointless cruise, the Germans raided Russian merchant shipping and shore bases.

For a long time, the Germans managed to send out cipher messages by radio to their forces in Africa without
having them broken. In fact, the British did not realize
that they were dealing with a cipher, for the sounds they
picked up were extremely fast and resembled static more
than anything else. In the end, quite by accident, a Brit-

1ST FIGURE | 2ND FIGURE

1st / 2nd	3	6	0	7	4	8	1	9	5	2
8	a	ä	ai	au	äu	b	c	ch	ck	d
2	e	ei	eu	f	ff	g	h	i	ie	j
6	k	l	ll	m, mm	n, nn	o	ö	p	pp	r
3	s	sch	sp	spr	ss	st	str	t	tt	u
7	ü	v	w	x	y	z	0	1	2	3
4	4	5	6	7	8	9	.	,	;	?
0	section	army	artillery	battalion	battery	brigade	bridge	division	railway	squadron
1	field	flight	air force	engineers	rifles	trench mortars	group	infantry	scouts	guns
9	cavalry	company	command	corps	men	morse	ammunition	officer	horse	pioneer
5	regiment	snipers	sappers	staff	tanks	train	truck	troop	watch	bombers

ish naval officer discovered that by slowing down a record of the sounds, he had quite clear cipher messages. The Germans had merely played the recording at very fast speed.

Later, German Army ciphers were nearly always practical and efficient. The German Army was the first to give a course in cryptography to young officers, and nearly every German officer is familiar with cipher use and practice. The majority of books on ciphers have been written by Germans. A typical German Army cipher is shown on previous page.

13

- **Transmitting Secret Writing**
- **Ancient Methods**
- **Hollow Teeth**
- **Using the Post Office for Espionage**
- **The Downfall of Spies**
- **Invisible Ink**
- **The Kent Case** • **The Black Chamber**
- **Telepathy and Hypnosis**

THERE is not much point in having useful information and a cipher or code in which to express it if you have no way of sending it. Men have shown as much ingenuity in methods of transmission as they have in the development of secret writing.

Going back five hundred years before the Christian era, we find in Herodotus: "When Xerxes planned to invade Greece, a Greek named Demaratus, a refugee at the Court of the King of Susa, warned his countrymen of Lacedaemon by means of a message traced on wooden tablets covered with wax. At first nothing could be seen on them and it was Gorgo, the wife of Leonidas the King, who discovered the stratagem."

One Greek ambassador in Persia used to shave a slave's head — under the pretext of curing him of some ailment or other. Then he would tattoo a message on the man's skull, let the hair grow, and send him to Greece to see "a doctor," who would, of course, shave the skull again and read the message. Other slaves were drugged and messages were then branded on their backs. On recovery, the suffering slave would be told to go to a certain place for treatment, where the message would be read and acted upon. Often, it would be in cipher.

Then, down the years, spies and agents sent messages concealed in the lining of coats, in wigs, in hollow shoe heels, in jewelry and even in hollow teeth. Madame Louise de Guichy, a noted French courier of Louis XIV's time, frequently carried secret information in her powder jar, and, on at least one occasion, a vital message was written on a fan she actually spread and used while being questioned by officers at the Dutch border.

In modern times, agents correspond with their headquarters in many devious ways. Even as recently as World War II, some of them used carrier pigeons, but this is a doubtful method at best for the birds can lose themselves or be shot down or can be attacked by another bird.

The quickest way is by radio, but this is more difficult than it seems, for an "outlaw" transmitting station can be tracked down by special apparatus and the station must keep on the move.

The postal services are useful except in wartime, when mail traffic between the belligerent countries breaks down. Mail can, of course, be sent via neutral countries, but this slows it up and many an important message has arrived too late to be acted upon.

Another disadvantage is that a letter is apt to be opened by a censor and any apparent inconsistency or oddity will arouse his suspicion. Some agents send secret messages contained within an apparently harmless letter. This can be done by spacing words and letters to give the dot and dash effect of Morse Code. The letter "i" can be dotted in and "t" crossed in many ways to send a message.

With a pin, an agent can prick a tiny hole under certain letters of a perfectly innocent letter; pinpricks can also denote the Morse Code. But this method would be unlikely to pass the eye of an alert censor. Cipher messages are often written under postage stamps, a fairly safe way of getting a message through, because an army of workers would be needed to steam off every postage stamp on millions of letters.

Not infrequently in the past, an agent has sent a piece of music to a contact in a neutral country, to be passed on to his headquarters in his home country. The secret message is contained within the quavers and crotchets of the music.

A spy in England could send a message by putting marks under various letters in the pages of *The Times* and send it to a friend in a neutral country, who would forward it to the spy's headquarters. This form of cipher is not difficult to break, but a large staff of censors would be needed to examine every newspaper and magazine for the telltale dots or pinpricks. Many years ago in England, postage charges could be afforded only by wealthy people. To send a letter from London to Scotland, for instance, cost 4s. (56¢), 1s. (14¢) for each hundred miles. Since newspapers were allowed to travel free, this was a wonderful opportunity for a man with a shrewd mind and thrifty habits. He could "write" a long letter to a friend or relation by simply putting a pencil dot above certain letters in a newspaper, which the Government then delivered free.

The counterintelligence agent, whose job it is to spot messages sent by enemy agents, is always suspicious about a letter which quotes prices, sizes and specifications. For instance, during World War I, a counterespionage agent found before him a letter to a firm in Sweden ordering razor blades. Sweden produces very fine steel products, including razor blades, and obviously such a commodity could justifiably be ordered in large quantities, but this particular quantity was very large. The agent checked the records and found that within a few months the writer in London had ordered from Sweden more razor blades than had been used in the British Isles in the previous three years. The man who had ordered them was watched, arrested and questioned. At his trial, it came to light that his razor-blade orders were secret messages in cipher. He was found guilty. He had not been as sharp as the razor blades!

Telephones and telegrams can be used by agents. Messages can be sent quickly by these methods, but a suspicious telephone line can be tapped, and a telegram intercepted by the censor — though this does not happen in peace time. In England, a line may be tapped in peace time, but only with direct authority of the Home Secretary. In the United States, regulations vary in war time and peace time. Each country has its own rules about line tapping.

A telegram was the downfall of the famous German spy, Karl Lody, during World War I. In England, Lody handed in a wire for transmission to Sweden. The girl clerk who accepted it read it when the sender had gone. AUNT PLEASE SEND MONEY IMMEDIATELY. I AM ABSOLUTELY BROKE. THANK HEAVEN THOSE GERMAN SWINE ARE ON THE RUN.

The girl was curious. If the man was "absolutely broke," why did he send such a lengthy message, with the pointless sentence about the Germans? She referred the telegram to the censor who thought it suspicious enough to pass to Intelligence. Lody did not last long after that. He was tried and found guilty of espionage. Nobody ever worked out what the appeal to "Auntie" meant; it was good cipher or code wasted by careless phrasing.

For many years, Germany had a special department, the Chiffrierburo, whose professional experts had to find new codes and ciphers, both complicated and safe, and to break ciphers used by other countries. They might have given Lody better training.

Probably the safest way of sending messages is by word of mouth, but this has obvious disadvantages. Contact has to be made and this can be highly dangerous; and it is difficult to memorize a lengthy, technical message.

The stitching of the threads on a suit or dress — arranged in Morse Code — can be a useful subterfuge. And, on at least one occasion, an agent's hair was cut in an elaborate way to pass a secret message. He was suspected because he did not wear his hat on a bitterly cold day!

For hundreds of years, spies have used invisible ink. For a long time, lemon juice and onion juice were used. They were invisible until the paper was heated and then the writing became clear: At least one spy used good-quality chemical invisible ink during World War II, but he was caught, nevertheless. His name was Herman Job and he came to Britain posing as a Resistance man newly escaped from an internment camp.

He had only one habit — that of writing several letters each day to "friends still interned on the Continent." He sent these letters through the Red Cross, but agents soon became suspicious of them and they were intercepted and examined. Herr Job had used invisible ink and cipher to write secret messages under the ordinary text of his letters.

Confronted with the deciphered messages, Job claimed that somebody must have tampered with his mail. Detectives searched his room but failed to find anything suspicious except a large bunch of keys. But why did he need so many keys when he had no locks on his closets and suitcases? The keys were sent to locksmiths who discovered that several of them had been specially prepared for espionage. The top (the bow) of some of these keys unscrewed and in the hollow stem was a chemical for invisible ink; the bottom (the web) unscrewed to show a plastic nib.

In 1940, Tyler Kent, cipher clerk of the U.S. Embassy in London, and in charge of the State Department code, used microfilm to betray vital British and American secrets to the Germans. He copied more than 1,500 cipher messages passing between the British Government and the American White House, in addition to reports sent by the U.S. Ambassador in London — then Mr. Joseph Patrick Kennedy — to the State Secretary, Mr. Cordell Hull. America was not then in the war but she was helping Britain in many ways.

Kent's spying came to light and caused a major upheaval. Because of his treachery, all U.S. diplomatic communications throughout the world were blacked out for several weeks until special couriers reached the various embassies with new codes from Washington.

Kent, who was only twenty-four, was dismissed from the diplomatic service. This enabled the British police to arrest him and he was jailed for several years.

Kent's microfilms were crude compared with later developments in this technique. The Ethel Gee spy ring, responsible for selling British naval secrets to the Soviet in 1960, reduced espionage messages to pieces of film the size of the period at the end of this sentence.

Every country has had its Black Chamber — a secret bureau for postal espionage — but Imperial Russia (before 1917) probably had the most efficiently conducted chamber. One of its chiefs, Karl Zievert, found a way to extract a letter from an envelope without tampering with the flap or wax seal. He invented a device that was merely a thin, round rod about the size of a knitting needle, and slit along half its length. He inserted this rod under the flap

at the corner, pushed it nearly across to the opposite corner until the letter caught in the slit. Now, delicately, he
wound the letter carefully around the stick and withdrew
it from under the flap at the corner. When the letter was
read and recorded, Zievert would replace it by the same
technique. He taught his operators to do this without
leaving a trace of their work.

The Americans had a highly successful Black Chamber
during World War I. Controlled by Herbert O. Yardley,
a great cryptographer, the Black Chamber scored many
victories; unfortunately, they are still secret. Eventually,
a politician decommissioned the Black Chamber because,
as he said, "Gentlemen do not read each other's mail."

Use of radio obviates difficulties with the Black Chamber. Just before D-Day — with the Allied Armed Forces
more security conscious than ever before — a German spy,
known to history as Hannah, was at large in London with
a powerful miniature radio hidden in a box of chocolates.
She enciphered her messages on a spool of magnetic wire
driven by a clockwork. To transmit, she merely pressed a
button and the complete message was reduced to one
brief *beep,* which could be picked up by the powerful
German receivers, and deciphered.

New methods of sending secret messages are constantly being explored. It has been reported that the American
firm, Westinghouse Electric, and also the U.S. Bureau of
Standards are conducting experiments in the use of telepathy in military communications. It is very likely that
the Soviet has also been busy in this field. Before World

War I, the Germans and Austrians had achieved the technique of locking a message into an agent's mind under hypnosis. Even the agent was unaware of the message until it was released from his mind by the correct signal. Other countries have since been working on this method.

14

• Mechanization: The Need for Speed

Now, like most things, ciphers and codes have become mechanized and many messages are ciphered by machinery. The cryptographer operates an electrical keyboard, rather like that on a typewriter, and simply taps out the message in clear. The machine automatically transforms it into cipher. But an error can cause him more trouble than a mistype can cause a typist. One unspotted mistake can result in the whole message being fouled.

The usual cryptograph machine has twenty-five discs fitting around a cylindrical shaft. On the rim of each disc, which is removable, is stamped a different disarranged alphabet of twenty-six letters. On the side of each disc is a number — 1 to 25 — and a letter — B to Z — so that they may be assembled on the central shaft according to a key word or a number.

There is an extra disc, blank, with a guide rule attached, which can be revolved around the shaft to serve the same purpose as a ruler when used with a multiple mixed alphabet table. The clerk can lock the discs on the cylinder in any way he wishes, according to the order predetermined by the key.

The only real advantage of the machine is that it adds to speed. The security of messages enciphered by the machine lasts from six hours to three days under service conditions. Generally, the Army changes its keys at irregular, predetermined intervals.

Machines are also used to decipher legitimate messages from agents. Ordinary apparatus is of limited value in deciphering "intercepts" — foreign messages — but it is used to count the recurrence of various groups. In a long message, perhaps thousands of words long, this mechanical aid can save much time.

Foreign languages are part of the challenge professional cryptographers face. The number of languages used by the various nations involved in World War II was astonishing. In India alone, there are nearly six hundred distinct dialects, and messages could be sent in any one of them. Then there were the Chinese dialects, the languages of the Pacific Islands — five hundred and ten in New Guinea and Papua — and all the many tongues of the Middle East and of Africa.

Despite the difficulties of foreign languages, skilled cryptographers take little longer to break a cipher. Before World War I, American experts cracked the "Purple Code" of the Japanese. With new electronic machinery, even the problem of language has been overcome. One machine can translate a foreign language into English with far greater speed than a human translator.

Today, speed is as vital as secrecy — speed in enciphering, speed in transit, speed in deciphering. Survival depends on speed and modern computers provide it. A complex computer can encipher a message with unbelievable rapidity. A computer can also be used to break a long and involved cipher in a short time.

Never before have nations become so security conscious. Machines and electronic computers notwithstanding, there is still the possibility of human error, so cryptographers are being more highly trained than ever before. Oddly enough, it is only in recent years that encipherers have been trained not to use standardized, stereotyped language in secret messages. There is a natural tendency in any organization, military or civil, to use the same old words and phrases, such as: "We have received your communication . . ." "In reply to your request . . ." "Yours of March 1 to hand . . ." During World War II, British Intelligence broke one enemy cipher quickly because the intercepted message began with the equivalent of "Thank you for . . ."

In service communications, it is sometimes very difficult to avoid repetitive mention of troops, ships and aircraft and many other special terms — and repetition is always dangerous. A naval enciphering operator might send this message: SIX TASTY FISH POSTED UNDER DARK COVER. (Six submarines have left during the night.) When this clear is enciphered, it would become very difficult for an enemy to understand even if he succeeds in breaking the cipher.

Major mistakes can be made, despite all precautions. In 1944, an American cruiser sent a cipher message to its headquarters in Hawaii; about an hour later, the same message arrived in plain text. The radio operator had been given both messages and had sent both, without realizing that they were identical.

The enemy had been made a present of the cipher but, within a few minutes, a fresh one was substituted and the information flashed to all units. On this occasion, no harm was done.

At secret schools, cryptographers are taught to destroy all cipher material, preferably by burning and then by scattering the ash. All enciphering must be done on a glass-topped table; on an ordinary table or blotter pad, an impression could show through. Cipher and clear must never be written on the same page. Typewriter ribbons must be used once only and then destroyed. Communications traffic must be kept at a constant level by sending null messages; a sudden build-up, in an emergency, would instantly arouse an enemy's suspicion. Any cipher material taken from an office must be checked out and checked in, and never taken out of the building. In fact, there is as much security in a cryptographical bureau as in an atomic research center. This is a measure of the importance of the science of secret writing.

15

- **Frequencies**
- **Occurrence of Bigrams**
- **Most Commonly Doubled Letters in English**
- **Useful Tips**
- **Most Frequent Trigrams**
- **Breaking Down a Cipher**

Frequencies

To become a cryptanalyst, you need patience and accuracy and an inquisitive mind. Mechanically, you need sharp pencils of two or more colors, quarter-inch graph paper, a ruler and an eraser. Always work in neat capital letters. No two people will solve a cryptogram in exactly the same way, but they should prepare for the job in a methodical way.

The first step is to decide whether the cryptogram is one of substitution or transposition. The letter frequency will show this. If the letters ETOANIRSH occur very frequently, in this order, you can assume that you are dealing with a transposition.

The repeated occurrence of low-frequency letters indicates that a message has been written in a substitution cipher. Here, you must make tables of frequency for single letters, digraphs and trigraphs. An important aid is the fact that cipher alphabets are usually based on some system or key. Make a point always of recording the cipher beneath the normal alphabet and you may detect valuable clues.

With a transposition cipher, you must find out how many geometrical patterns the cipher will fit. For example, a message consisting of seventy-two letters can be written in ten different patterns; two lines of thirty-six letters (both vertically and horizontally); 3 x 24 (both ways); 4 x 18 (both ways); 8 x 9 and 9 x 8; 6 x 12 and 12 x 6.

Transposition ciphers are more difficult to solve than substitution, because patience and perseverance are necessary to plot through dozens of possible combinations of letters before we find the correct one.

The first signs of success in breaking a cipher are the appearance of common letter combinations. But astute cryptographers have frequently made things more difficult for the analyst by sending messages in phonetic spelling or in "crazy" spelling. MI RAIDEEO IZ BROWKEN. WEN WIL I HAV NU BITZ. This clear is not so clear and, when enciphered, would give an enemy analyst even more trouble to decipher than usual.

When an expert analyst has two messages of the same length, he can break the cryptograms with comparative ease, no matter how complicated the enciphering method used.

Letter	Frequency of Occurrence in 1,000 words	Letter	Frequency of Occurrence in 1,000 words
E	591	M	114
T	473	U	111
A	368	G	90
O	360	Y	89
N	320	P	89
R	308	W	68
I	286	B	65
S	275	V	41
H	237	K	19
D	171	X	7
L	153	J	6
F	132	Q	5
C	124	Z	3

But even an expert, attempting to decipher a secret message of which he does not know the key, must know the frequency with which letters occur in English.

It is not necessary to memorize all these because you will always have frequency tables to which you can refer, but the letters can be grouped in the following way for easy reference:

1. E
2. T
3. A, O, N, I, R, S or O, A etc.
4. H
5. D, L, F, C, M, U
6. G, Y, P, W, B
7. V, K, X, J, Q, Z

The same order does not necessarily apply to other languages, except in the case of E. In English, French, Spanish and German, it is the most common letter. In Italian, it is I and Polish, Z.

Occurrence of Bigrams (two letters)

Letters most frequently occurring together are:

TH, HE, AN, RE, ER, IN, ON, AT, ND, ST, ES, EN, OF, TE.

Most Commonly Doubled Letters in English

LL, EE, SS, OO, TT, FF, RR, NN, PP, CC, MM, GG.

Useful Tips

More than 50 per cent of all English words end in E, S, D or T.

More than 50 per cent of all words in English begin with T, A, O, S or W.

F as a terminal generally ends the word "of." G as a terminal generally ends a word with an "ing" ending.

Most Frequent Trigrams (three letters)

THE, ING, CON, ENT, ERE, ERS, EVE, FOR, HER, TED, TER, TIO, VER.

Another aid to deciphering is the table of letter frequency in relation to the position of the letter in a word.

Initial letters: T, A, O, M, H, W, C, I, P, B, E, S
Second letters: H, O, E, I, A, U, N, R, T
Third letters: E, S, A, R, N, I
Final letters: E, T, S, D, N, R, Y, G,

When dealing with proper names, the endings provide more of a clue than letter frequencies. This can be observed in the French language, in which 8 per cent of the proper names end in ER or IER — *e.g.*, Fournier, Mercier, Boulanger; 7 per cent in ON, sometimes with a third letter — *e.g.*, Champion, Dupont, Leblond, Lamond; 6 per cent in AU (perhaps with a third letter) — *e.g.*, Boileau, Rousseau, Moreau, Nadaud, Callaux.

Of German names, 25 per cent end in ER, and 6 per cent in the syllable, MANN — *e.g.*, Hermann, Dollman.

Endings most frequently found on English surnames are: SON, TON, ER, ING (S), LEY, FORD, STON (E), MAN, OCK, BY. Oddly enough, there are many more of these endings than ITH (Smith).

Breaking Down a Cipher

Suppose you have no idea of the method of encipherment used for a message, but you must break that message. It is: OG XGGH YWXGM QTEGXRZM WT OG IKXXWR VTWIGGH RW TWYG WX OGHXGSHKM.

Is it substitution or transposition? The cryptogram consists of more consonants than vowels and the commonest letter of all, E, appears only once, so we can be certain that some form of substitution cipher was used. Setting to work methodically, we make a letter count of the cryptogram. We put down each letter of the alphabet and tick it each time it occurs.

A occurs — times		N occurs – times	
B	—	O	8
C	—	P	–
D	—	Q	1
E	1	R	8
F	—	S	1
G	11	T	4
H	4	U	–
I	2	V	1
J	—	W	7
K	2	X	7
L	—	Y	2
M	8	Z	1

If we need it, we now have real proof that we are dealing with a substitution cipher. An ordinary transposition could not use the letter x seven times in fifty-three letters and the vowels only six times collectively. Also, it seems evident that the original word divisions have been maintained, which is always a help to the analyst.

The digraphs OG and GG are worth underlining, preferably in color, so that we can tell the number of occurrences. OG recurs three times and GG twice.

Much cryptanalysis is trial and error, so we will try substituting E for G. We write our partial solution, as follows:

```
1    2     3      4        5   6    7        8       9  10   11
?E  ?EE?  ???E?  ???E????  ??  ?E  ??????  ????EE?  ??  ???E  ??
    12
?E??E????
```

Very few two-letter English words end in E and we know from our tables that many words begin with w, so we will substitute clear w for cipher o. This gives us:

```
1    2     3      4        5   6    7        8       9  10   11
WE  ?EE?  ???E?  ???E????  ??  WE  ??????  ????EE?  ??  ???E  ??
    12
WE??E????
```

w and x appear seven times each and could stand for T, A, O, or N. Logically, we would try T and A in our workings, but I can save you some labor on this occasion and tell you this would lead nowhere. Next, if we substitute clear o for cipher w, we would get:

```
1    2     3      4        5   6    7       8       9   10   11
WE  ?EE?  ?O?E?  ???E????  O?  WE  ????O?  ??O?EE?  ?O  ?O?E  O?
    12
WE??E????
```

The two-letter word ?o catches the eye, since this is most likely TO. It could be GO, SO, DO, NO, but TO is much more frequent.

Assuming R stands for T in the clear, we have:

1   2   3   4   5   6   7   8   9   10   11
WE ?EE? ?O?E ???E?T?? O? WE ????OT ??O?EE? TO ?O?E O?

12
WE??E????

We have not yet tried the high-frequency letter N. The
letter x appears seven times and could easily stand for
clear N. We now have:

1   2   3   4   5   6   7   8   9   10
WE NEE? ?ONE? ???ENT?? O? WE ??NNOT ??O?EE? TO ?O?E

11   12
ON WE?NE????

Look at the first two words, WE NEE? What else could
the second word be but NEED? Substituting D for the H of
the cryptogram, we find:

1   2   3   4   5   6   7   8   9
WE NEED ?ONE? ???ENT?? O? WE ??NNOT ??O?EED TO

10   11   12
?O?E ON WEDNE?D??

Very often, a cryptogram at this stage of breaking has
one word which stands out in some way. Here, it is the
last group. A glance at the dictionary will tell us there is
only one word beginning WEDNE — WEDNESDAY. Having
deciphered three more letters (we already had the D),
we can proceed with our filling in:

```
1   2    3      4      5  6    7      8      9
WE NEED ?ONEY ???ENT?Y O? WE ?ANNOT ??O?EED TO

10  11      12
?O?E ON WEDNESDAY.
```

Group 3 now suggests MONEY, since it is unlikely that anybody would be sending a cipher message about HONEY, so we can substitute Y for clear M, which brings us to:

```
1   2    3      4      5  6    7      8      9
WE NEED MONEY ???ENT?Y O? WE ?ANNOT ??O?EED TO

10  11      12
?OME ON WEDNESDAY.
```

Obviously, now, Group 7 is CANNOT. HE CANNOT TO HOME? But if the first letter of Group 9 is H, the second letter of Group 5 is also H, which would give us OH and an ejaculation of this type in the middle of a cipher message is highly improbable. Perhaps T in the cipher stands for R, another letter of high frequency. T appears four times.

```
1   2    3      4       5  6    7      8
WE NEED MONEY ?R?ENT?Y OR WE ?ANNOT ?RO?EED

9   10  11      12
TO ROME ON WEDNESDAY.
```

Little cryptographical ability is necessary to complete the analysis. WE NEED MONEY URGENTLY OR WE CANNOT PROCEED TO ROME ON WEDNESDAY.

The message was enciphered using the St. Cyr Slide,

with two alphabets in straight sequence but reading backwards, underneath the clear alphabet.

This is a simple message, but the principle remains the
same for difficult ciphers. Method is needed — plus a little imagination.

16

- **Definitions**

ACROSTIC: This is a text in which a set or several sets of letters, *e.g.*, the first or last letters of a line, form a word, phrase or sentence, when read in sequence.

ANAGRAM: A word, phrase or sentence formed by transposing the letters of another word, phrase or sentence, *e.g.*: *dose* is an anagram for *does,* and *dear* for *read.*

BILATERAL: Consisting of two letters.

CIPHER: A method of secret writing or cryptographic writing that systematically disarranges the normal order of the letters of a plain text, or that substitutes other letters, characters or symbols for the normal alphabet.

DIAGRAM CIPHER: A transposition cipher that employs diagrams, pictures, sketches, photographs, etc., to conceal the plain text.

CLEAR: The communication before it has been enciphered or encoded.

CODE: (1) A system of signals for communication by telegraph or semaphore. (2) A cryptographic system by which groups of letters are substituted for syllables, words, phrases or sentences. (3) A secret method of communication, other than cipher, by which one person transmits information to another person.

CRYPTANALYSIS: The science of deciphering cryptograms by analysis and deduction, without prior knowledge of the key to the plain text.

CRYPTOGRAM: A text in code or cipher.

CRYPTOGRAPH: A mechanical device for enciphering and deciphering.

CRYPTOGRAPHY: The science of secret communication.

DECIPHER: To convert an encoded text into plain text.

DECODE: To convert an encoded text into plain text.

DIGRAPH: A group of two letters.

DUMMIES: Letters used to complete a group. *See* NULLS.

ENCIPHER: To convert a plain text into cipher text.

ENCIPHERMENT: A text in formal or informal cipher. In a *formal* cipher, the letters, numbers or symbols are written in even group lengths, usually of five units. In an *informal* encipherment, the natural length of each word in the plain text is preserved in the cipher text.

ENCODE: To convert a plain text into cryptographic text by means of a code book.

FREQUENCY TABLES: The most important tools of the cryptanalyst, Frequency Tables show the relative frequencies of letters, pairs of letters, trigrams, syllables and even of words in normal text.

GRILLE: A paper or·mesh with apertures through which a secret message can be read after the grille has been placed over the text in which the hidden message has been written.

IDEOGRAPH: A pictorial representation symbolizing a thing or the idea of a thing.

KEY: (1) A prearranged word, phrase, sentence or number that determines the steps to be taken in enciphering and deciphering. (2) A cipher alphabet.

NULLS: Numerals, letters or symbols placed in a text, either to complete a group or to fill out a pattern, usually to make it more difficult for a cryptanalyst to discover the hidden message.

ONE-PART CODE: A code book in which the plain-text words, phrases or sentences are arranged in alphabetical order with the equivalent code groups also in alphabetical order beside them for the purpose of encoding and decoding.

PALINDROME: A word, verse or sentence that reads the same from right to left as it does from left to right, e.g., level.

PATTERN: The geometrical form in which the text is written in transposition encipherments.

SIMPLE SUBSTITUTION CIPHER: A cipher in which one letter of the clear is represented by one and always the same letter, figure or symbol of the cipher; *e.g.*, if the clear is STAY AWAY and each letter is represented by the one preceding it, the enciphered message will be: RSZX ZVZX.

SIMPLE SUBSTITUTION WITH SUPPRESSION OF FREQUENCIES: A cipher in which each of the very common letters, such as E, is represented by several letters or symbols; *e.g.*, the message is PLEASE HELP, with each letter represented, as before, by the one preceding it in the alphabet, except E, which is denoted by 1, 2, 3. The cipher will read: OK1ZR2 G3KO.

DOUBLE SUBSTITUTION CIPHERS AND TWO-STEP CIPHERS cannot be briefly defined and are explained fully in the text.

TRANSPOSITION CIPHER: One in which the letters remain the same as in the clear, but are rearranged to a particular pattern.

TRIGRAPH: A group of three letters.

TWO-PART CODE: A code book with two sections: an encoding section in which the plain-text words or phrases are arranged alphabetically with the code groups beside them, not alphabetically arranged; and a decoding section in which the code groups are arranged alphabetically but their meanings are not.

VARIANTS: Two or more letters of characters that represent plain-text letters.

17

• **Some Cryptograms to Test Your Skill**

• **Solutions**

THESE cryptograms are fairly simple; a really difficult one could take months to break down. All are based on types of ciphers described in the book. If you cannot decipher them, you will find the types of cipher, key words and solutions on the following pages. Try not to give up too easily, but if you are forced to give up, work backwards from the solution to see how each message was enciphered.

1. BGKSM RQBUS QYRQX JTDBU SGSOB MGRTQ YJMBQ
   XQJIS DJQBR QSVBQ YQYSR DSIQW

2. IPF LFE PVO TOD QLR UOF VDY DCM KEH KSY

3. EYAPTGY CTEASNO NILPEAU OCSYDDA TERORNR
   AVEREIE

4. 241 213 726 247 192 226 231 062 697 229 818 131
122 981 213 211 292 169 719 229 129 232 298

5. RUWRJ EEWHT MRNCW BAAWJ BOBHF RFRQV

6. ZKXQB RXUYF ZLYXW KLVPY VVDJZ VXQGL WRQWR
DJYQW Z

7. HEQ EJP WJJ SUF JVX PQI VUD SXJ JEU HWS POJ FBO
TRG CDA

8. $;\pounds!?;-\frac{1}{8}=\pounds+!\frac{1}{8}-\%\pounds\frac{1}{8};/\frac{1}{8}?.(\frac{3331}{4448}°\pounds/\frac{1}{8}?;)\frac{1}{8}''$

9. LRPEMNII IOEDMSRM AJHIITUU FETASROS LCRTNUYT
LTOEOCEH IWYLITVA

10. A–GUR B–OBTTXPQC C–VF D–IWLFSLWN

11. YTRHTI RUOTAF MYGHTE LLIEVW IFMOFR NITEME

12. 31433 32411 41414 24133 43443 14333 12513
43434 43454 35411 24511 45442 44513 41112
51000

Solutions

1. Simple Substitution by Double Parallel Alphabet.
Key word: Rhapsody. One null. Solution: Imperative
that you give me firm authority to negotiate with the
agent.

2. Playfair Substitution. Key word: Prime. One null. Solution: Rendezvous at the quay at midnight.

3. Simple Transposition: Seven lines of six letters, first line written backward. Solution: You are in danger. Destroy papers. Leave city at once.

4. Very Simple Numerical Substitution. Alphabet numbered in reverse, 26 to 1, then grouped in three's. Solution: Contact headquarters in person for further orders.

5. Vigenère Table. Key word: Major. Solution: Funds sent care of Paris Post Office.

6. Julius Caesar cipher, with suppression of frequencies. x, y and z are used in this order every time an e occurs in the clear. Where x, y and z occur naturally (that is, when they represent letters three places before them), they are underlined. Solution: When you receive this message send it on to Agent e.

7. Vigenère system using a key number — 5432. Message grouped in three's; one null. Solution: Cancel the order unless you hear from me by Monday.

8. Transposition cipher; Chinese style. The clear, of fifty-six letters, was written down in eight columns of seven letters. Solution: I must have your instructions immediately or the project will fail.

9. Substitution cipher; Porta Simple, using four alphabets: Normally, each word of the cipher would not be labelled with the key letter. Solution: The password is sentinel.

10. Double Transposition. The clear was arranged in six lines of six letters. The lines were transposed in the order 654213 and, finally, the columns were transposed in the same order. Solution: Form Five will meet in the gym at four-thirty.

11. Greek figure substitution cipher. Three nulls. Solution: Conrad did not confess so you are quite safe. (Would *you* have been more successful than the Chevalier de Rohan?)

Index

Aegospotami, Battle of, 28
Alfred, King, 12
Argyll, Duke of, 63
Arte of Shorte, Swifte and Secret Writing, The, 55

Bacon, Francis, 45, 47, 48, 49, 50, 51, 52
Bardin, General Charles, 73
Bazières, Commandant, 69, 70, 71
Bilateral Cipher of Francis Bacon, The, 48
Black Chamber, 65, 119, 120
Booth, William, 49
Bright, Timothy, 55, 56
Brühl, Count, 65

Canaris, Admiral, 19, 20
Cardano, Jeronimo, 35, 53
Chappé, Claude, 73
Charlemagne, Emperor, 12
Charles I, King of England, 60, 63
Charles II, King of England, 63, 71
Charlestown, 78
Chiffrierburo, 117
Cicero, 27, 28
Cipher:
    Autoclave, 42
    Baconion, 45, 46, 47
    Chinese, 88, 144

Combination, 93, 95
Double Parallel — Alphabet, 86, 95, 143
Double Transposition, 90, 92, 95, 145
Great, of Louis XIV, 58, 76
Greek figure, 31, 145
Grille, 35, 36, 139
Julius Caesar, 27, 144
Lord Wolseley's Square, 85
Multiple mixed alphabet table, 123
origins of, 16
Pig-pen, 44
Playfair Square, 82, 83, 84, 110
Porta Simple, 89, 144
Porta Table, 39, 41, 89
Quadrilateral Alphabet, 61, 62
St. Cyr, 81, 135
Trithemian, 32, 35
Two-Step, 92
Tyronian, 28
Vertical Parallel, 90
Vigenère, 40, 41, 42, 43, 76, 144
Zodiac Alphabet, 32, 33, 34
Cipher Clock, 98, 99, 100
Code, Morse, 14, 78, 79, 115, 117
Purple, 123
codes, commercial, 12, 14
symbol, 100, 101, 102
Condé, Prince of, 57, 58

D-Day, 19, 20, 21, 120

de Bulonde, General, 70, 71
de Catinat, Marshal, 69, 70
de Guichy, Louise, 114
della Porta, Giovanni Baptista, 38, 41, 44
de Louvois, François, 70, 71
Demaratus, 113
de Rohan, Réné, 22, 23, 24, 25, 145
de Truaumont, 22, 23
de Vigenère, Blaise, 41
Donnelly, Ignatius T., 47, 48

Elizabeth, Queen of England, 45, 48, 53, 54, 55
Essex, Earl of, 48

Fabyan, Colonel George, 50, 51
Frederick, Elector of Brandenberg, 63, 64, 65
Frederick II of Prussia, 65
Frequency Tables, use of, 24, 25, 127, 128, 129,
    139, 130, 131,

Gallup, Elizabeth, 48, 49
Gee, Ethel, 119
Gendron, Commandant Victor, 69
Gifford, Gilbert, 54, 55
Graham's Magazine, 74
Great Cryptogram, The, 47
Gross, Professor Hans, 101, 102

Hall, Admiral Sir Reginald, 108, 109
Hannah, 120

Hart, J. G., 47
Henry III, King of France, 41
Henry IV, King of France, 56
Herodotus, 113
Hull, Cordell, 119

Ink, invisible, 118

James I, King of England, 63
Jellicoe, Admiral, 108
Jilinsky, General, 106, 107
Job, Herman, 118
Julius Caesar, 27, 144
Jutland, Battle of, 108, 110

Kasiski, Major, 75, 76
Kennedy, Joseph Patrick, 119
Kent, Tyler, 118, 119

Langie, André, 26
Lee, Arthur, 72
Lody, Karl, 117
Louis XIII, 58
Louis XIV, 58, 59, 63, 69, 114
Lysander of Sparta, 28, 29

Macbeth, J. C. H., 11
Magdeburg, 107, 108
Mary Queen of Scots, 53, 54, 55, 60
Mazarin, Cardinal, 58

Meyer, Lieutenant-Colonel Hellmuth, 20, 21
Monmouth, Duke of, 63
Morse, Samuel, 78, 79

Napier, General Sir Charles, 75
Napoleon Bonaparte, 66, 73
Naseby, Battle of, 60

Osman Pasha, 80
Owen, Dr. Robert Dale, 48
Pepys, Samuel, 63
Pitman, Isaac, 56
Poe, Edgar Allan, 74, 76
Polygraphia, 32

Redl, Colonel Alfred, 103, 104
Rennenkampf, General, 106, 107
Richelieu, Cardinal, 58
Room, 40, 108, 109
Rossignol, Antoine, 57, 58, 59, 63

Seward, Henry, 78
Shakespeare, William, 45, 48, 49, 50, 51
Shorthand, origins of, 55, 56
Shorthand Alphabet, Bright's, 55, 56
Sir Francis Bacon's Cipher Story, 48
Skytale, 29, 30
Smith, John, 63
Some Acrostic Signatures of Francis Bacon, 49
Szek, Alexander, 109

Tannenberg, Battle of, 107
Trevanion, Sir John, 61, 62
Trithemius, Abbot, 32, 34, 35
Tyro, 28

Viète, François, 57
von Hindenburg, General Paul, 107

Wallis, Dr. John, 60
Walpole, Horace, 47
Walsingham, Francis, 53, 54, 55
War, American Civil, 44, 76
  Boer, 82
  English Civil, 60
War I, World, 109, 116, 117, 120, 121, 123
War II, World, 21, 114, 118, 123, 124
Wolseley, Lord Garnet Joseph, 85

Yale University, 78
Yardley, Herbert O., 120

Zievert, Karl, 119, 120
Zimmerman Telegram, 108, 109